One who lives in love ful[fills]
the will of God. - 20

9780874861034

Happiness of the senses does not bring peace
of soul. - 93

Marriage... teaches us to know God and hold fast to him.
- 119

See Isaiah verses on p. 123

126-127. We do not "make Church." Church comes
to us from God.

Revolution - the opposite of evolution - 157

It is a matter of the spirit of which we come before God. -185

Col. 1:9-10 ! Knowing God for living for God.

Love and Marriage in the Spirit

Emmy Arnold, Eberhard Arnold's wife and life companion and our house mother, brought a motherliness and womanliness to the most important, formative years of the beginning and early growth of our community life. For Emmy's eightieth birthday on December 25, 1964 we, her brothers and sisters and our families, wish to dedicate this book with deep gratitude to her.

Love and Marriage in the Spirit

Talks and Writings by Eberhard Arnold

The Plough Publishing House
Rifton New York 1965

Copyright © 1965 by
The Plough Publishing House
Woodcrest, Rifton, New York

Edited and translated from the German at the
Society of Brothers
Woodcrest, Rifton, New York

Library of Congress Catalog Card Number: 64 - 24321
Printed in the U. S. A.

CONTENTS

Introduction	ix
Love Divine and Human	1
On Woman's Calling	28
The Nature of Woman and of Man	33
Marriage and the State	47
The Mystery of Unity	58
Faith and Marriage	64
Conscience and Responsibility	67
The Bond of the Spirit	70
Responsibility, Desire, and Love	80
The Promise	103
Engagement	114
The Three Grades of Marriage	118
Marriage in Unity	129
Marriage a Symbol	132
What is God's Love?	137
Love Redeemed	144
Christ the Head	160
Appendix	225
Glossary	233

INTRODUCTION

Love is Jesus' innermost being and nature. "A new commandment I give to you," He said on the eve of His crucifixion, "that you love one another; even as I have loved you, that you also love one another." Love will be the distinguishing mark of Jesus on His followers. "By this all men will know that you are my disciples, if you have love for one another."[1] For the followers of Jesus, this love becomes both the goal and the way to the goal. This love is their living witness.

Marriage, in a unique and special way, points us to the deepest truths about love. Every human being has experienced love from father or mother, brother or sister or comrade. In this love he has experienced the desire of one person to wish and do the best he can to care for, protect, make happier an other. In the love experience of marriage, there is the added, unique quality: unity. As it is said in Genesis, "They become one flesh."

In the love of Jesus for His disciples, and in

[1] John 13 . 34, 35

the love of His followers one for the other in the early Church in Jerusalem, this quality of unity was decisive and integral. Jesus makes unity the touchstone of witness and of faith, when in His last prayer with His disciples, He asks, "that they may all be one; even as thou, Father, art in me, and I in thee, that they also may be in us, so that the world may believe that thou hast sent me."[1] In witness to the power of the Spirit poured out on the early Church, we hear "the company of those who believed were of one heart and one soul, and no one said that any of the things which he possessed was his own, but they had everything in common."[2]

Marriage, and especially weddings, become for Jesus and His disciples a joyful example and symbol of the love and the unity of love that ignite their hearts. Reciprocally, the purity, faithfulness, service, self-sacrifice, and the deep-going unity of the love of Jesus for His Father and for His disciples become a living guide to husband and wife in marriage.

Eberhard Arnold lived his life and gave his life in witness to Jesus' love. His experience of unity with others in following Jesus penetrated

[1] John 17 . 21   [2] Acts 4 . 32

Introduction xi

heart and mind and also the reality of material life. The power of Jesus' gospel of love was revealed in community of work, community of goods, community of table.

For Eberhard, too, weddings in the church-community were an especially rich and joyful occasion to speak of the nature of man, and of woman, and of true marriage, and at the same time a living opportunity to witness to the uniting power of God's love. The talks and essays in this present volume are selected from the times when he spoke as word leader of the little community, or from the writings in which he addressed himself to what he considered one of the main life-problems of young people.

Words, especially religious words, have been made cheap by hypocrisy. In the reaction against hypocrisy, it is no service to truth and genuineness to cheapen actions as well. Yet in our western world in this century, acts in sexual relations are becoming cheap. The personal harvest can only be pain, suffering, and the deadening of conscience, sensitivity, and the capacity to love. We hope that these words of Eberhard, which have a committed life behind them, can give an assurance and point a direction in our time to hearts that are unsure and faltering in purity or in faith. With Eberhard, we can only confess and affirm, and we want to stand behind it with our lives, that true marriage is pure, faithful, committed, just, and loving. Anything else is counterfeit.

There is an appendix and a glossary for any who want to know something of the setting of the talks and understand some of the terms used that are not in common use. In the little book, *Eberhard Arnold*, Emmy Arnold his wife contributed a summary, "Eberhard Arnold's Life and Work," and Emmy Arnold's book, *Torches Together*, is a fuller description of Eberhard's life and background and the first seventeen years of the Bruderhof, as the little community came to be called. The reader can learn in those two books about the life experiences out of which the thought and feeling of this present volume emerge. Here is only the briefest summary.

Eberhard Arnold was born in Königsberg on July 26, 1883. He and Emmy Arnold were married in 1909. In his youth and early adult life, Eberhard was deeply influenced by a lively evangelical movement, and later by the German Youth Movement. During and just after the First World

Introduction xiii

War, he was one of the secretaries of the German Student Christian Movement. (Chapter nine, "Responsibility, Desire, and Love" was written in response to questions and problems he met in working with students.)

The spontaneous, the genuine, the love of nature, the concern for the oppressed that were characteristics of the early Youth Movement were welded to a deep-going Christian commitment in Eberhard and Emmy. Together with friends from widely ranging backgrounds they faced the bankruptcy of war and the need all around them in war-racked Berlin. Starting from a fresh examination of the Sermon on the Mount they were led to a decision to give up personal property and live a life of brotherhood with community of goods, in faith and for service to others. Their venture began with their own family and two or three close friends in the village of Sannerz, near Schlüchtern, in Hesse.

This was the beginning of a great adventure in Christian community. Most of the chapters of the present volume express the thoughts of Eberhard and at the same time speak for the little community.

Over the years the community ardently sought

contact with other similar groups, and Eberhard sought the threads of primitive Christianity through history. In this way the community discovered that the Hutterite Brothers, one of the Anabaptist groups from the time of the Reformation were still living in community of goods in North America. Eberhard spent about ten months among the Hutterites, a time that was a deep-going enlivening experience for both groups. The Bruderhof became acquainted with the rich heritage of their writings from the sixteenth and seventeenth centuries. Chapter twelve, "The Three Grades of Marriage," and chapter four, "Marriage and the State," are talks based on parts of Peter Rideman's *Confession of Faith*, one of the most important Hutterite books, dating from 1545.

Through studying the background, the reader could in this way find one or another influence on Eberhard's speaking and writing. The dominant, burning force, however, behind the words of this book is the life in Christian church-community itself. Jesus tells us that He came to set the world on fire, "... and how I wish it were already kindled!"[1] "... I have come to

[1] Luke 12 . 49

Introduction xv

bring division."[1] Every attempt to establish a beachhead under the banner of God's kingdom rouses violent opposition. A committed stand for purity is attacked by impurity. A witness to Jesus' command to love our enemies brings attacks from front and flank: in the early thirties the little community was attacked repeatedly by the Nazis (who finally seized the land and buildings and drove the community from them in 1937), while at the same time Eberhard grieved that close friends attacked and deserted him for his feeling that the Nazis, too, must be shown love. Absolute fealty to Jesus alone perplexes or angers the government and alienates champions of the class struggle. As each new member gives up his property to free himself for a life of brotherhood and true justice, immediate relatives and friends often respond with suspicion and anger.

The power behind any bondage is only really revealed when the one bound begins to struggle to free himself. In the struggle for freedom from them, the powers of violence, coercion, property, and impurity become revealed for the demonic powers they are, and Eberhard refers to them so. The little community went through great

[1] Luke 12 . 51

struggles. And yet the greatest struggles of all were fought out in the heart of each brother and sister. There, in the heart, grow impurity, greed and anxiety, violence, hatred, pride, and self-love.

All is shared in church-community. These struggles are also shared, and Eberhard who was dearly loved and trusted and who had been asked to be the word leader of the little group, knew these struggles intimately. It is from the fire and dust of battle that these talks and writings emerge. Emmy Arnold did the main work of selecting for this book. The deepening faith can be felt in them. The last chapter, "Christ the Head," is perhaps the most all-inclusive expression of this faith. We wish from the reader only that you read with your heart open.

Eberhard died in 1935, and the little movement staggered under the loss. The community was more deeply wounded at the time than any but a few realized. The Bruderhof is now called the Society of Brothers in England and America where our four communities now are. It is a precious and wonderful thing for each of us to have known Eberhard as a brother and Emmy as a sister, either directly or Eberhard, for many of us, through our brothers and sisters who lived

Introduction xvii

with him. It means a lot to us to be able to publish some of his words.

The only other book in English which contains his work is a little volume, mostly of excerpts from letters and talks, titled, *Eberhard Arnold*. *Children in Community* has in it several quotes from things he said about children and childhood, and a collection of shorter quotations are selected for daily reading in the little book *Inner Words*. We hope that this present volume will only be the first of several. The next one will be a collection of Eberhard's talks on the occasions of Advent and Christmas, along with talks by Christoph Blumhardt and Alfred Delp.

At this writing, in October 1964, in the United States we are intensely aware that young people are risking their lives for freedom, brotherhood, and justice in our Southern states. Opposing them are not only the long-standing strongly entrenched injustices of racial discrimination, but also new voices unleashing fear, suspicion, and hatred across the whole land. More than ever, we want to give our own lives that "the world shall become a consecrated place for the spirit of community.... We are infinitely far away from this goal. We have to trust in the spirit of life which is the spirit of love and unity and solidarity; trust in the spirit of life and justice which alone is life. In this trust we shall attain, through freedom and beyond equality, to brotherliness and true love."[1]

It is our hearts' longing that all who in a lonely way now fight for justice, as also for peace, purity, freedom, and love — that they might find joy in the fight, brothers to stand at their side, and the radiating source of life, light, and love. Here is one of Eberhard's poems, expressing our faith:

> In rhythmic joy the members swing,
> And hearts, close bound, with gladness sing,
> Purity lives!
>
> Sparks of joy, at first alone
> In stillness sunk,
> Will soon unite and flame as one!
>
> None can quench such burning flame,
> And hearts renewed find love again.
> Daylight dawns!

Arthur Wiser
Oak Lake community

[1] "Love Redeemed" chapter sixteen of this volume.

LOVE DIVINE AND HUMAN

DICKENS portrays in his *Christmas Carol* a rich old merchant in whom all but the last spark of love had died. His life had been ruined because he had given himself over completely to earning money. Nothing but coldness came from him, as if he were a man without a heart. This deathly atmosphere was so tangible about him that no child or beggar on the street would think of asking him for the time of day or of approaching him for the slightest help.

In deathly loneliness he lived a purely commercial existence without any human relationships whatever. He had even sacrificed the love of his youth to the idol of money. Any pure hope was consumed in the striving to assure himself recognition and success in the bourgeois world, until at last every noble feeling was extinguished in the craving for financial gain. A man of established fortune, he had become a soulless being.

His life was so completely turned away from the community of men that his death was merely the confirmation of a long established condition. Only if the spirit of his youth were once more to awaken, would his lonely coldness and emptiness give way to God's warmth. Only if he gave himself with new faithfulness to the old longing for life and love, if he left behind everything that had killed life and love, would the message of Christmas bring him new life.

No one can live without love. A person without love is an aging and dying, in truth, a dead being. Where love sickens and degenerates, the innermost life is poisoned. The affirmation of life is found only where love unfolds without restraint. Anyone who allows love's ardent urge and longing to go unused is suffering the same priceless loss of his most precious possession as all those whose most sacred powers are squandered into a dirty drain.

The life question for all young people is love. Each one feels that love is his destiny. There are many who, in hours of anxiety, fear the love life. Among youth, too, there are weak people who flee love like the plague. Love appears to them as a glowing hot fire which their fearful

Love Divine and Human 3

souls want to avoid; others, who are no more fireproof, come too close to the blazing fire. They allow the house of their lives to be destroyed in a smoldering fire. Their outward person deteriorates because they let their inward humanity go to ruin. Like a dying crater they burn out their hearts in impure passion instead of letting the sun's eternal powers glow through them, passing on to others pure light and genuine warmth.

For most people, love is a labyrinth in which they cannot take a step without blundering. They have not discovered the secret of how to guide the living stream into the right channel. Perhaps they feel that all love must end in God, just as all rivers flow into the ocean. They realize that much water trickles away or evaporates instead of finding the way for which it is destined. Basically, they want nothing but the fulfilment of their own being and God's being. Yet they lack the living vision to separate the pure, original force of love from its weakened forms.

In our language there is only one word for all the degrees of love, even for all its sick and deviant forms. In this simplicity of expression the mystery of love lies hidden. This mystery suggests that love is the one final thing about which everything moves that has life, to which everything is related that signifies hope, by which everything is sustained that breathes living power.

Nature's powers of attraction all derive from the same mystery of love. In the great universe, the rhythmic order of the circling constellations represents a monumental image of love. Not a single plant grows without love. No animal, however small, is hatched or born without love. Nowhere do people come together, nowhere are living beings procreated and born, unless a spark of love unfolds its life force. Our language does not distinguish between *love* and *love*, to indicate the healthy and the sick relationships between body and soul and between soul and spirit. The Greeks saw a clear difference between three forms of love: passion, which is possessive desire; Eros, which is the attraction of body and soul; and finally Agape, which is divine love, God's all-embracing love that gives itself to all.

In our circle of friends we are frequently asked how these three spheres of love are related to one another. Some are inclined to deny any essential difference between possessive love and the affection of people for one another on the level

Love Divine and Human 5

of their souls and bodies. Others want to separate sharply the holy love which pours out riches, from contact with Eros. Their radical opponents, on the other hand, insist that since there can be no radiance of love without erotic energies, God's love does not exist at all.

Anyone who is out of contact with religious life must judge in this latter way. Anyone who has experienced how God's love has been literally poured out over him has felt overwhelmed by its radiance and submerged completely and forever into it. Such a one can never be dissuaded from the certainty that all experiences of love, of whatever kind they may be, are but single rays or impure and distorted reflections of this one unending sun of life. He has become sure that God's holy love alone is the essential in the love life. Therefore, the one important question relating to love is whether it belongs to this center of life, or whether it has strayed away from it.

It has been pointed out that in the different areas of the brain, the areas of religious experience and of the experience of love are neighboring. Here lies a deep symbolism which points to the ultimate truths, for "God is love, and he who abides in love abides in God, and God abides in him."[1] Even the most degenerate and besmirched feelings of love have something from God hidden in them. However, their deterioration, like a corroding poison, consumes what is of God down to the last fragment, so that a person who is drowning in the flesh no longer has an eye for God and His love.

Anyone who spends the energies of his love in the intoxication of the senses deprives the neighboring centers of the brain of their vital power. He exhausts and ruins his feeling and spirit for the life of God. He becomes dull to the noblest impressions that come from the heart of God. His eye, created for the light, can find its way only in the dark. No one who is impure is able to see God. The inward vision of the soul springs only from the purification of the heart. Agape, divine love, is God's pure vision. It is at the same time, the flooding of our entire life with the pure power of God which is love. This love knows no lust or possessiveness. Most people know only of the Eros of desire, which in its most destructive forms, as ever-changing lust, exchanges one possession for another. Nevertheless, the important

[1] I John 4.16

Love Divine and Human 7

question is whether we can win through to an Eros life ruled by pure Agape.

On the first impression, the two ends of a straight line seem to move away from one another into infinity. However, one who sees into the mystery of existence knows that they will meet in infinity; the straight line which is visible to us has to be regarded as an infinitely small portion of an infinitely large circle. The straight line which is visible in ordinary life represents in our picture the area of the Eros life. In the visible world of time and space, men, who are spiritual beings, can find no relationship to one another without experiencing an attraction or repulsion of soul and body. This is the sphere of the emotions, the holding of hands, the meeting of eyes, the striding together arm in arm. This is the fellowship in word and song, in hiking and sport; it is friendship and fellowship in joy and sorrow, in faith and hope; this is the life community of mankind without which we cannot live.

In all this life God is present. The essence and basis of all life and community is Agape, the love that comes from God and leads to God. Agape is the love that never ends and knows no bounds. Agape is the revelation of the transcendent in the immanent. God is love. He who remains in love remains in God, and God in him. Therefore, the line of human love relationships which is visible to us flows into the community of God, into God's very heart.

The love of two people, or the community of a bond of friendship, or a community of believers, finds its fulfilment only in His inexhaustible and everlasting eternity. In these ultimate heights alone can men find the strength to let love flow through their whole lives and to let all their gifts be unfolded. Only in this atmosphere can they gain the purity to radiate a love free from the greed of possessive desire in the world of Eros. Finally the intoxication of the senses is replaced by the ecstasy of the divine Spirit, which the human viewpoint must assume to be asceticism. Eros is completely under the rulership of Agape. The all-embracing Spirit replaces the separated possessive will.

At one point the line of love ends in the world of the eternal and endless. "But joys all want eternity — want deep, profound eternity!"[1] Faust at first wants to go exulting toward the

[1] Nietzsche, *Thus Spake Zarathustra*

Love Divine and Human

moment of joy in physical love: "Ah, still delay — thou art so fair!" But finally he finds the true fulfilment of his longing in the enduring work of building and preserving the community of humankind. In all the ways in which Faust's power of love seeks fulfilment, Goethe sees the power of Eros which, at the close of the book of Faust, leads him to conclude: "The Eternal Feminine leads us upwards." If we follow the tangible, ascending line of love to infinity, life leads us to God. If we follow the line of love exclusively toward God, in the direction of the pure Spirit, toward the highest destiny, we shall attain inner wholeness and unity. Only the one holy symbol of a sole unity of two allows us to press forward with impunity, also in the opposite direction, into the infinity of the ultimate depths.

At each moment we are touching the world beyond. Each moment is a breath bringing us the air of eternity. Each moment brings us in contact with love. In the holiest moments of total physical union we are submerged in the world beyond. We are lifted out of our own limitations and placed into the closest community with the spiritual world. Oneness given between two beings endowed with soul and spirit is an event in the world of eternity. The more intense the experience of love, the stronger and more effective becomes the influence of the transcendent world upon our lives.

The decisive question of our destiny, therefore, is that of the inner nature of our love experience, above all, that of the nature of the spiritual powers with which we have allied ourselves. One may be unaware at such moments whether he has joined with the powers of darkness or with the light of God; yet he will come to realize it by the effects these moments inevitably entail. One who goes to the harlot becomes one flesh and one spirit with her. One who enters into the eternal oneness of two before God and in God, experiences the blessing of this sacred mystery in his own body and spirit.

God has compared His covenant with His people and the unity of Christ with His Church to this union of betrothal and marriage. The one eternal Christ is the single object of the devotion of His Church; He kindles in her all the powers of love and of the Spirit. In the same way, complete unity is given in marriage, a unity which awakens and unfolds all the powers of manhood and of motherly womanhood. Mar-

Love Divine and Human

riage, which is the will of two to create something beyond themselves, is a participation in God's creative power. In our spiritual life this participation should awaken all our energies for God's essence, His will, and His love to all. Baptism, the symbol of dying and of rising again to the unfolding of a full and pure life, can take place only once; it is absolutely unrepeatable. The same is true of marriage to the one person who is given to each of us for the fulfilment of all his and all our potentialities in life.

Thus our love life becomes our destiny in the most serious sense of the word. It may either hurl us into the hellish abyss of demonic self-destruction where what is holiest and best in us is lost; then Eros has become satanic desire and lust. Or it may lift us to the pure heights of God's light where we find the fulfilment of our destiny and calling; then every sphere of Eros has been taken possession of by God.

Now, some may ask about those who can never find the happiness of unity between two in body, soul, and spirit; here we stand before the mystery of a most noble calling of God's love. An impulse from the world of the eternal powers is needed for people to penetrate to a decision which makes them completely happy, people who had been deeply unhappy in their disappointed or frustrated desires. Those who long for the garden of love which is closed to them and who rattle its locked gates cannot attain this mystery.

It may be, however, that to some the way of marriage is barred by bitter experience. There may be others who, due to an inverted inclination, do not feel drawn to the opposite sex. They all can find an unsuspected wealth of happiness in their lives if the holy decisiveness of God's love breaks through within them. None of love's energy should be wasted or go unused. No life power shall be suppressed. It is essential to rise up out of the gloomy chamber, out of the smoky city, out of the valley filled with fog and sickly vapor, so that the vision becomes free, the heart opens wide, and the lungs breathe pure air. It is essential that all energies be converted into highest and purest powers so that they can develop unbroken and unrestrained.

There is a complete freeing from the Eros of selfish desire when Eros is wedded in everlasting faithfulness to Agape. Whoever can be liberated once and for all from the sexual in this way be-

Love Divine and Human

longs to the happiest of men. He is able to love more than others because his entire time and strength are free, because Agape, God's love. dominates exclusively his relationship to all men. The heavenly kingdom can break in upon earth more freely through him because the stream of his love moves in one single direction. In this sense Jesus spoke of those who are eunuchs for the sake of the kingdom of heaven, and Paul spoke of those for whom it is better not to marry because their special mission requires a special preparation.

The person to whom the way to the one pure marriage seems to be closed must not estrange himself from life and love in bitterness. He must not stifle the best in himself. He must never give himself over to desires which cannot awaken and unfold all the aspects of the best in him, above all, that of God in him. Rather, he has received the higher calling in which all his powers of love are kindled and revived by the generous, sunny love of God. They are not spent in possessive desire but devoted exclusively in the enthusiasm of lavish giving. Here, love to many and all comes into its own, love that wants nothing for itself but is fulfilled in giving.

In reality, every human being, whether given the capacity for the love of man or the love of woman, whether married or unmarried, is placed before the same question at important moments of decision. In reality, we all live in a certain asceticism which we have found to be the highest, all-embracing, and life-affirming love of God. More and more this asceticism says "No" to possessive desire. It has made a final separation from the sexual domain. Its decision is for the one pure life of divine love into which the Holy Spirit alone is able to submerge us. Here all our living together is flooded with white light. Hand in hand in pure joy, boys and girls, men and women, stand before the great gate which heaven has opened upon earth for them. They lead one another to their highest calling, to that life of love which gives away all possessions and strength without ever losing itself.

We should not be surprised that such a pure community in crystal-clear, wholehearted affection is so often believed to be impossible, for the love life of many knows only the impulses of physical desire. Certainly, even in the ugliest sensual desire there lies hidden a divine spark of love's higher powers. However, where the

Love Divine and Human 15

covetous will is the characteristic of the love life, of the whole thought life, and of the deepest hidden longings, love remains ruled by the animal and demonic realms of our being. In this condition no one attains the heights of true humanity and fresh youthfulness to which every human being, without exception, is called. In this lowland the emotional life proves incapable of allowing love to mature to faithfulness, which alone can be the fulfilment of a fellowship of love.

The highest and ultimate love, poured out over us as eternal power, wants to penetrate and to affirm our physical powers of love. This love cannot tolerate our enslavement by animal sensuality. It does not want us to be dependent on the state of the body. It wants to lift us into the highest spheres of divine freedom and divine purity, out of which and toward which moves all that is living.

We rejoice about those powers of Eros that cannot be mistaken for sultry eroticism. The Greek Eros does not represent mere physical sexuality, but communal experiences of the soul which belong to a relatively pure atmosphere. Yet the purest air of love is the breath of the

Spirit which goes out from Jesus; Socrates or Plato could only sense this. The forces which are to be felt in the youth movement are powers of Eros in a new form, powers in which freer air, fresher wind, a wider view, and a purified joy prevail. The tender emotional life of innermost fellowship in love has mastered the gross physical drive of brute sensuality. Young people have become aware that all relationships of body and soul between people are always and everywhere relationships of love. They dare to rejoice in these love relationships in jubilant affirmation of life. They dare to comprehend in these relationships the only possible shaping of community and of life as a whole. Only here and there has this emotional upsurge of the most hidden powers penetrated into the regions of the Spirit and to Christ.

As the youth movement branches out more and more, it becomes clear as day that all ways which lead away from Christ must lead into the mire. It is evident that the forces of Eros without the power of Agape cannot lead to purity. A shameless nudity cult has desecrated the mystery that can only belong to the unity of two people, which is a sacred symbol. It is an im-

Love Divine and Human

mediate need in the youth movement to keep a clear distance from those who have escaped from the prostitution of the big cities only to be just as miserably enslaved by other forms of possessive desire.

To the clear-sighted the domain of Eros is distinctly divided into two opposing camps. The straight line which is visible to us, a portion of the eternal circle of love, runs downward here into the darkness. Just as surely as the sympathies of body and soul can be fully dominated and kept pure by the love of God, they can be enslaved by Eros in vacillating, unfaithful, and emotionally sordid desire. To the extent to which the youth movement falls prey to this Eros life of lust, it is lost and finished. Insofar as it finds joy in the Eros life of pure Agape, it can be called to something great for our people and for humanity. The youth movement is standing at a crossroads where neither Buddha nor Lao-tse nor any other Indian or Chinese, but in truth Christ Jesus alone can help.

This hour of decision for the youth of today[1] is regarded with serious apprehension by orthodox Christian groups. These groups have repeat-

[1] 1920

edly experienced how quickly a crude sensuality drowns out the tender movement of the soul; because of this, they are unwilling to believe that a new, freer, and purer spirit is at work in new forms of living. Nietzsche's reproach to Christianity was that it had poisoned Eros, had taken away its innocence. From this, he said, Eros died. This crushing accusation applies to the general lines of development in church history. A strong inclination toward a purely negative asceticism has become noticeable in the youth of today who struggle against the dangers of degeneration and defilement. But Jesus did not want this.

Jesus had no distrust of life; He joyfully affirmed all life's forces which are illumined, penetrated, and ruled by God's love. He gave a high place to marriage and its inviolability. He honored marriage by discerning its desecration in the impure thought and the covetous look. Jesus gave His Church brother-love as its sign, love that is Agape, in community of table and of prayer and openhearted discussion. In His own life He showed how the purity of love embraces all people without servile anxiety and works everywhere without being stained. Jesus loved the rich young man when He looked at

Love Divine and Human

him as He alone could look and challenged him to give away all his riches and to follow Him. He loved John, who himself called attention to how he leaned against His breast at table. Though denounced by His enemies, He allowed those to come close to Him who sought a freeing from their sick sensuality in love to Him. Women of ill repute were allowed to kiss His feet and to wash and dry them with their hair, or to anoint His own hair. And even on the cross He gave His mother a son and His beloved young friend a mother.

In His Spirit, Jesus brought a final transcendence of the Eros life; seen from a false perspective this could be misunderstood as a stifling of emotional relationships. This transcendence is the revelation of the love of God free from desire. Eros of itself is not free of covetous desire. Therefore, it is not free from jealousy of others in their loving and being loved. It is not free of boastfulness and conceit. It can injure tenderness and purity of feeling; for it still seeks its own. Eros does not stand up for justice and truth because by its very nature it remains partial. For this very reason, it cannot of itself become one with that attitude toward life which believes all things, hopes all things, endures all things. Eros can be poisoned, sicken, and die; for it is of this world. Plato's *Symposium*, the loftiest eulogy which world literature has devoted to Eros, unveils its sickness to anyone who looks more deeply.

God's love is eternal and imperishable. It is the greatest and final revelation on our earth of God's universe. Greed and vanity, possession and property must perish because they are worthless for the eternal. Even the highest gifts of language, knowledge, and prophecy belong to time and will perish with it. Love, however, is simply life itself, life in every sense, full and everlasting life. Jesus has revealed to us that love is the greatest of all things. One who lives in love fulfils the essence and the will of God. For he lives in God. God lives in him. There is no other community with God than that of love. Faith is alive only in love. Faith without love is nothing. If anyone brings forth the clearest proclamation and the purest teaching but has not love, he is less than noise and smoke.

The warmth that comes from God's heart cannot be produced in any laboratory, by any decree, or by any organization. No friendly

Love Divine and Human

efforts or zealous benevolence can imitate this genuine gold. Whoever has felt this unique life power radiating from the aged or from the wheelchair of a cripple knows that this power is independent of the physical freshness of youth. It is life itself. It is the one primary force, the original power of the deepest source. Wherever we meet this life power it is the effect of a cause, the cause of all being. *Omne vivum ex vivo.* Love begets love. He loved first who himself is love. Only out of this first cause are we able to love.

Hence the love that is Agape, in contrast to the intrinsically sick Eros, bears the character of Him who literally pours it out over us. It knows no bounds of space and time. It destroys nothing. It is the strength of unconquerable perseverance. It is steadfast faithfulness and therefore is equal to every task.

Agape, as genuine kindness, alone knows what is right for each person in every situation because it is free of the passionate stirring of naked Eros, which seeks by all the wiles of jealousy to win or to hold what it supposedly loves. It clothes the energy of our love in the divine light of inexpressible purity, which can never be unseemly or ugly and can never injure the modesty or sensitivity of the soul. Being God's love, it is free from all inflated arrogance, from all pretense, from all presumption for its own advantage.

Agape seeks and demands nothing for itself because it lives completely in the object of its love. It knows nothing of rights, for its nature is to abandon and forget the standpoint of rights, to find its happiness in giving. Vanity and envy are beneath it, therefore it can never be made harsh, never be thrown into excitement, never be provoked to bitterness. Agape sees the essential nature and potentialities of the other one; thus it does not take into account what may still be evil in him. Yet it has nothing to do with injustice. It concentrates its joy completely on the real, the genuine, the true in the soul of the other person.

Agape sees through everything which still delays the holy calling of a soul. It has the strength to be a protection, to endure and ward off all dangers that threaten to obstruct a person's destiny. It can do this because it is one with faith and hope, because it is completely in God, because it lives in the final fulfilment of man's future. For this reason alone, it is able to stand firm everywhere and to endure everything. Agape

Love Divine and Human

is present where the unfolding of the full powers of manhood is given in Christ, never where there is merely passing effervescence or superficial enthusiasm.

Anyone who has read the sublime song of love in the original text as Paul wrote it[1] knows that this was his expression of the Greek song of praise to Agape. Those who feel something of this love arise in their hearts, experience across the centuries and millennia the aliveness and timelessness of the same spirit working directly in them. Slowly the light dawns within, so that we begin to sense how life could be opened to us by this perfect love. We long for this unspeakable happiness and feel what it means for all men to encounter Him who radiates this life.

No founder of a religion, no philosopher or moralist has lived this love as Jesus did. We can only reach God's heart if we encounter Jesus. In Christ the love of God became manifest. The Word became flesh. Jesus came down into the life of physical and emotional relationships. At all times He was the kingly giver, the man who gave riches.

Jesus knew only the crystal-clear, purified love

[1] I Cor. 13

of the kingly service for which He came into this world, not in order to make men His servants but to serve and give up His life. He revealed the love that forgives everything and gives everything. He revealed the love that includes enemies as well as friends, the love that allows no injury to any opponent or his property, much less to his physical life. Yes, He showed that love is not limited by possessions or property. In Him, love is the unconditional and absolute for which we all long. This love could never accept being frustrated by outward circumstances.

The love of Jesus is forever and is boundless, or it is nothing. There is no other characteristic of Jesus and of a Jesus-life than love. Therefore, Jesus said that by the love that His own would have for one another the world would know that they belonged to Him. He knew himself to be one with the original source of love, therefore He established love as the characteristic of His being.

The cross of Jesus is the ultimate gift of God's love. Here our loveless and lovesick lives come to an end. Here begins the new life of divine justice which can be no other justice than that of love. Before, we gave ourselves to the service

Love Divine and Human 25

of degenerate and degrading ways of love; now we give ourselves to the service of justice and perfect love which belongs to all.

When we find this deepest and all-embracing fulfilment of our need of love, when our hearts are filled with powers of love as the sun is filled with flames of fire which it hurls out into the farthest reaches, then we are set free from possessive desire. The forgiveness and cleansing which Christ gives to our degenerate love life goes hand in hand with the outpouring of the flood of His love. Whoever is surrounded by this spirit will only feel at home in the atmosphere in which Jesus himself lived. In Christ we experience how God loves us; then we no longer expect to be loved by men but seek life's happiness in love toward men.

This ultimate and highest love which we can attain is of the Spirit and is the highest calling of the Spirit. In this direction alone lies the solution to the problem of life. Where a man struggles with his erotic passions, not a spark of love's energy shall remain lost, no life power be suppressed. On the contrary, he should look into the heart of God at each moment of his life and open himself to Him so that he may live out love,

God's love, in every area of human relationships. He must allow the Eros life to be ruled completely and exclusively by Agape, thus conquering selfish desire through its overflowing power.

The community of life which grows in this way cannot allow anything to remain outside of its life circle. It holds fast to everything that belongs to life. Whoever has surrendered to this glowing sun cannot withhold any area of his life from it; again and again he will return to it with all that he is and has. When the spirit of love came over the first Christians they became one heart and one soul. They greeted each other with the holy kiss. They shared in the breaking of bread and had all things in common. Among them the meaning of brotherhood in the common life, of freedom in the pure Spirit, became revealed. They had become one family. In them was revealed the mystery of organic community among men.

The all-embracing Spirit is the unity of all freed spirits. He effects the freedom of the soul's powers which now flow toward one another, no longer dependent on sympathy or antipathy or on the conditions of the body. The Spirit rules over the uniting of men; all of life's goods come

Love Divine and Human 27

under His power. Wherever freedom, purity, and the love of God reign, wherever Christ lives in individuals, wherever His Spirit unfolds all gifts and powers, there grows a living unity. This unity is to be seen as one body.

ON WOMAN'S CALLING

I BELIEVE that our modern attitude has mistaken the calling of woman. What we find in the Hutterian movement over the centuries must certainly not be confused with the subjection of woman; they have really discovered the true expression of her nature.

What is woman's noblest possibility? When we recognize the noblest quality of woman we shall have to reject the false quality. The Bible in both the Old and New Testament, as well as history throughout the ages, shows us that woman is given a divine love; it reveals that the light of the Godhead, shedding love as it flows forth, streams out from her. God's light constantly streams from her in deep and tender love.

Man's nature, again taking the noblest quality, has something of the volcanic which breaks out in decisive moments, pouring out its glowing lava. It is a fighting nature which wields the sword of the Spirit, which carries the fight into the open with prudence and forethought, with deliberation and complete clarity, yet with challenging, storming, driving energy which presses forward into battle.

In man there is the eruption of solar flames, in woman the flowing, harmoniously spreading light of the sun. These differences are vital and must not be distorted. Although it is a matter of light, these differences are more definite than those between two distinct constellations.

Woman is predestined to a way of love which is not given to man. Man seeks people at the moment when he knows a challenge must be made, when he knows that they need to be shaken and awakened and their hearts changed. Woman is quite different. Her love is steady, faithful, constant. She will give her motherly, sisterly help in a deeper way to those already familiar to her, rather than to the stranger and newcomer, while a man will pour out his energy particularly to the stranger and newcomer.

Of course, not every man has received the same gifts. Gifts are bound to vary. But for us, work — any kind of work — is the expression of love. Man with his great muscular strength or his exceptional gift of a comprehensive outlook is called to especially hard outward struggle. The gifts of leading the battle, of government, of leadership, and of steering the ship of war are allotted to the man because they are not in keeping with woman's nature. The man's gifts are not more valuable; they are of a different kind.

The kinds of work which fall to woman do not usually demand great muscular strength of her. Rather, they are in keeping with her loving, loyal, quiet nature. Woman's task is to be loving and motherly, dedicated to preserve, protect, and keep pure the circle of those who are close to her; to train, to foster, and to cherish them. It will be a loving, cherishing, and motherly task. The task can be expressed in different professions and different activities. It may lie in the spiritual, cultural, or practical area, or perhaps in an area intermediate between them. This will be different in every case, but if she remains a true woman then this love and care for the circle entrusted to her will always be contained in woman's calling.

Under no circumstances is man's work of fighting and pioneering, which brings him in conflict with the outside world, to be more highly prized

On Woman's Calling

than this cherishing, this inward and creative giving of life and depth to the church-community. There is no difference at all in worth; there is only a difference in calling. If it should be given to us to affirm woman's tasks and not wish for her the work of administration and direction, then our common life will be a happy one. This difference in calling is something like the difference between one who works with his head and one who works with his hands. It is a completely middle-class attitude for the intellectual to despise the laborer. If this were our point of view we would be quite unable to live together. Nor is the reverse attitude possible. Both are equally wrong. The right way is to give the intellectual an opportunity to take part in manual work without his individual ability being lost. The manual worker should also be given an opportunity to take part in mental work without his special ability being lost. The one who does mental work should be as highly appreciated as the manual worker, and the one who does manual work should be as highly appreciated as the mental worker. This is the solution to the problem. I believe we can come to this through an understanding of the Body of Christ.

A woman must not say, "If only I were a man." Nor must a man say, "If only I were a woman." Nor must the mother say, "We must weep when a girl is born." Nor should the handy man say, "I would now like to be in charge of the bookkeeping." The eye must not say, "I want to be an ear," or the ear say, "I want to be an eye." Each one should be aware of his own particular task.

In the knowledge of the Body of Christ we shall find the true solution to the problem of woman's calling. Those who are unmarried can unfold their gift of love all the more strongly and extensively if it is not concentrated on one human being. However, when the true order of marriage is given among us every woman will have her true place. She will order, talk over, and agree upon all things with her husband in an inner way. She will have a very strong influence on her husband. She cannot, however, exercise the chief authority or a parallel authority. Then the unmarried woman, too, will not desire or demand the chief authority but will concentrate all her love on God and on those people who seek.

THE NATURE OF WOMAN
AND OF MAN

MEETING with the community, four newly received novices—Arnold, Gladys, Kathleen, and Winifred—raised questions concerning the relationship of man and woman. Eberhard Arnold lead the meeting and spoke for the community in his answers and comments. This is a shorthand record of the meeting.

ARNOLD: We would like to ask about man and woman, about their natures and the difference and the relationship between them as these things are set forth in the four points of the Hutterian article on marriage. Here the man is regarded as the head of the woman. He appears to be placed higher. Are they not equal? Then it is said in the four points that the wife is to follow the husband in all that is good and godly, and she is asked whether she wants to do this. Why is this question asked only of the wife and not of the husband? If there is full unity and if we are concerned with unity then the wife cannot be under a moral force; *compulsion* would be saying too much, while *influence* would be saying too little. They must complement one another perfectly. They stand side by side as equals. We feel that the only difference between man and woman is purely biological. They are utterly different, but out of this difference they complement one another perfectly. The wife is necessary to the husband and the husband is necessary to the wife. At times the husband is superior to the wife. As beings in themselves they are equal.

GLADYS: The difference between man and woman is more than just a biological difference.

EBERHARD: Is there such a thing as a merely biological difference? Behind this difference something else must lie, something more essential, otherwise the biological difference would not exist either. The biological difference is only the outward aspect of a deeper difference.

KATHLEEN: I have represented the same point of view as Arnold until today, that the difference

The Nature of Woman and of Man

between man and woman is merely a biological one.

ARNOLD: The question is, what is the real difference between man and woman? Looking at your practical living together and your mutual relationships, it seems to me that our relationship to one another is exactly like yours.

WINIFRED: Before I came here I also used to think that the difference was only biological. Since I have been here I feel that something much deeper lies behind it; I feel that this difference between man and woman has a much deeper basis than the biological one. The question as Arnold and Gladys and Kathleen have put it is only a question of personalities. The real question must be asked and answered from a deeper source.

EBERHARD: There is something much deeper than the question of the development of the feminine personality.

WINIFRED: I suspect there is something deep here which lies behind the whole of life, something which I cannot yet name. I do not want to speak about it before I understand more about it.

GLADYS: I too feel that it is not just a question of personality and that the answer to this question of the difference between man and woman is the key to the polar tension between the masculine and feminine principles.

EBERHARD: The feminine principle lies much deeper than the biological aspect of woman. If we believe in the divine and creative Being, then we know that something deeper and more essential lies hidden behind every outward appearance. As truly as God is creator of all things, so surely there lies hidden behind every outward, visible difference a more profound, invisible difference. It has been pointed out, and rightly so, that this difference is not a difference in worth. Woman's nature cannot possibly be ranked lower than man's, or to express it the other way around, man's nature cannot possibly be set above that of woman. This is completely out of the question.

We must, however, come to recognize the particular spiritual nature of woman; we must come to recognize woman's spiritual being and nature in its essence. It must be understood that the spiritual nature of woman also exists independently of the body. Thus the material body is merely the shape and form given to this spiritual being. A sculptor gives shape and form to some-

The Nature of Woman and of Man 37

thing already given to his spirit. To express it as Plato did, the feminine principle existed before the body of woman.

We must search for a woman in the history of mankind, a woman in whom we can recognize this feminine principle. In their writings the Hutterians have recognized in Mary the mystery of womanhood and motherhood in its deepest sense. What did Mary do? She believed the living word that God spoke to her. She was not troubled by the fact that God spoke this living word to her through a messenger. She felt that the Holy Spirit came to her in this word. She received the word. She received the Spirit and said, "Behold, I am the handmaid of the Lord; let it be to me according to your word."[1] He who commanded her was God.

Thus the eternal Word was not ashamed to receive flesh, body, and form from Mary in order to become man. And most important of all, God's eternal love became man. God's eternal truth received earthly form.

To continue then: The old Hutterian writings, with a right understanding of the New Testament, say that Mary is the image of the Church.

[1] Luke 1 . 38

Mary is the mother and the Church is the mother. The mother is not a visible church of some particular creed, composed of human beings here and now. No, the mother is the city above, the invisible Jerusalem. The mother is the city of the kingdom of heaven.

Our Bruderhof is not Church through being composed of believing and loving people or through the sum of the believers. The Bruderhof *becomes* Church whenever the Holy Spirit, the Jerusalem above, comes down upon us; whenever the Church above unites us in the Holy Spirit.

The reality of the motherly Church exists before life in community represents the Church here and now. Or, in other words, the reality of the Holy Spirit brings the Church down to us who believe. Thus the Church is given through the Holy Spirit.

The Holy Spirit comes to us as He came to Mary, and thus we become children of God's Church. The Church is the mother and we are her children. This is the mystery of our deep fellowship, of our community which extends to the whole of life.

Now here is something astonishing. The place

The Nature of Woman and of Man

assigned to woman in the first creation is the same as the place assigned to the Church in the new creation. The example and image for both is Mary. Woman in her spiritual nature is like the Church. Such is the place of woman in marriage. The woman who does not marry because of a special calling has this same place.

The highest thing that can be said of a human being is that his nature is similar to the nature of the Church. There can be nothing higher for a human being. It is the nature of the Church to bring life into the world in the fullness of community with the Holy Spirit and in motherly strength, to give form and reality to new life in this world and to do these in keeping with God's will and with His being and His word. This is woman's place. It is given to her by Christ and by the apostolic word.

If we know women who are truly womanly, we realize that the essence of woman is the heart, the motherly spirit, the innermost feeling for all that is holy. Womanly nature has the gift of feeling, tasting, sensing, and absorbing the atmosphere of the Holy Spirit. It has the intuition which senses the atmosphere surrounding a thing or person even before the person has expressed by a word or sentence what he thinks. The genuine woman, the believing and loving woman, has a very deep perception of the radiations and stirrings of soul and spirit and thus in particular of the Holy Spirit.

All that has been said here about Mary, about the Church, and about woman and the womanly nature is not a matter of the mind. Naturally, this is not to say that woman does not have a mind. But the important part of the true woman is not the mind or the intellect. This is a good thing. The curse of the nineteenth century was that it acted as if the mind alone were the spirit and soul of man. This is the ugliest monstrosity that the materialism of the nineteenth century has brought forth. The materialistic way of thinking gave rise to this wrong emphasis and this wrong concept of human nature, which also encompassed the relationship between husband and wife.

We must now speak of the spiritual nature of the man. You will by now have an inkling of what the apostolic word of the New Testament means in saying that the man is to be the head. This does not mean that the head rules over the body by force or tyrannizes it. This is not the

The Nature of Woman and of Man 41

case in our bodies either if we are true men. I would resist with all my might against my relatively stupid brain being the master over my whole life. The head has its significant place in the body but it is not the tyrant of the body. Heart and head must go together.

Thus we must not confuse the significance of the place of man in marriage and in the order of creation, we must not confuse man's nature with what is called the intellect, although from a certain point of view it can be compared to the intellect. The spiritual nature of man is much more than the manifestation of human intellect. We feel it in this way: In God's all-embracing Spirit He shall give and entrust to the man the substance of His thoughts, His plan and design. To man as the head, then, the guiding thoughts of the Spirit are entrusted for administration and leadership. In His revealing Spirit, God entrusts to him His historical and superhistorical plan. God's plan, the movement of the centuries toward the coming kingdom, is to be revealed and entrusted in a special way to the man. To express this in Biblical words, God's kingdom as the revelation of the plan of the Spirit is entrusted to the man in particular. Man is called to apostolic mission which is indissolubly bound together with the Church. This is man's apostolate, a mission that shows the way and clearly sets forth the cause and its direction. This is the man's nature and calling.

We have already spoken of how we understand the life of the Church and what the Church is. The apostle stands within the Church. Regardless of whether he is Peter or Paul or John, he demands nothing of the Church that is inwardly alien to the Church. Out of the inspiration of the Holy Spirit, the apostle speaks guiding and clarifying words and thoughts of God.

These thoughts of the Spirit which the apostle speaks are alive in the heart of the whole Church. What he says is said in the name and authority of God, and at the same time what he says is said in the name and authority of the whole Church. What the apostle furthers is always God's cause; what he furthers is always the cause of the Church.

This, then, is the relationship of the head to the Church. The head thinks in the Spirit; through the word of the Spirit, the head expresses that which is always present though unspoken in the whole Church. When the right man is lacking,

The Nature of Woman and of Man

the man who can put it into words, everything is still there and working in silence but it will not be given clear expression. An apostle without the Church would be a sad and impossible thing; so too the Church without an apostle is sad and impossible however faithful the individual members of the Church may be.

Therefore, having held up Mary as the example of womanhood, we now see the apostle as the example of manhood. Even though there is scarcely one individual husband who can be an apostle or any one wife or woman who can be like Mary, yet man's task and place in accordance with his spiritual nature is and remains this and no other. The question of whether woman has received the nature and spirit of Mary and man the nature and spirit of the apostle is all the more pressing because we see so many human beings who are far from living in this way. Yet we have the faith that all of them can become open to this calling and can go at least a little way in this direction. All can do this through the inspiration of the Holy Spirit, through Christ. In the Holy Spirit, Christ the Head is the image of man and Christ the Body of the Church is the image of woman.

GLADYS: Once one has started to go on this way, one can no longer turn back. At times this is a terrible thought; at other times it is a wonderful thought. When Jesus asked the apostles whether they wanted to leave Him they said, "Lord, to whom shall we go? You have the words of eternal life."[1] This is our situation now.

ARNOLD: I have much more of a feeling now about the relationship between man and woman. I did have a vague idea about it before, but I haven't quite found my balance yet.

EBERHARD: It is startling and overpowering. The calling that has come to you is overwhelmingly great.

ARNOLD: If one were able to understand everything rightly and do everything correctly, then God's kingdom would already be fulfilled here and now.

EBERHARD: God's kingdom comes to us in Christ and in His Spirit. It is grace. The life we have left behind appears quite impossible to us now. Yet on the other hand it is so difficult to live in the right way. We have to accept what is given to us by the Holy Spirit.

WINIFRED: Before I came here I used to have

[1] John 6 . 68

The Nature of Woman and of Man

difficulties in this matter of woman's deep responsibilty. However, these difficulties disappear when one puts everything in the context of the great cause.

EBERHARD: As long as it remains a specialized and isolated question nothing can be solved, nothing at all!

WINIFRED: That was my difficulty.

EBERHARD: That is what ails the world. All questions have become isolated questions and thus none of them can ever become clear. The secret of God's kingdom is polarity and universality. All questions become one question. That is marvelous!

KATHLEEN: I find it hard to say what I feel because what we have spoken together is so unusual for me. I feel that my life is like an empty vessel held out open to be filled by God's Spirit.

EBERHARD: You may know from the arts and from the history of civilization that the posture adopted in prayer used to be quite different from what it is nowadays. In present-day churches and Christian communities it is customary to pray with hands and fingers folded together, with head bowed and eyes closed. In early Christian times the posture in prayer expressed what

Kathleen has just said. Hands were raised like cups; like empty vessels they were lifted toward God so that He might fill them. This is the prayer of one who knows that he is empty and believes that he will be filled. Surely it will soon be given to us, too, to come before God in this way.

MARRIAGE AND THE STATE

THE WORD marriage means unity. Unity is at stake. It was for unity that Jesus sent out His apostles. This unity is a unity of justice, of love, and of joy; it is a unity of peace.

Unity is an all-embracing power which lives in God's heart. It has not yet attained victory throughout the world. The mass of the people still live in disunity. They are enslaved to the violence of mammon, of lying, discord, hostility, hatred and injustice, the violence of mutual opposition and destruction. They do not yet want the joy of the perfect love of the Spirit, the joy which places unity above everything. In spite of this, unity is something firmly established in the mightiest Spirit. But this Spirit does not force unity upon anyone, for in His kingdom He wants to have free spirits who come to His community in complete freedom of will. A dedication that is unfree and forced means less than nothing to Him. Because of this He leaves men in their terrible unhappiness unless they turn around of their own free will, seek His spirit of unity, and found His community of peace.

The deepest unity is in God. It is a hidden unity, a unity which is not yet visible throughout the world. It is a unity that will come to the whole world in His Spirit, His wind, His breath. Wherever there are people who are ready for this unity of His Spirit, there unity will be established in complete community. This complete community grows out of the innermost union of God's heart with those hearts that are bound together. It is founded in the unity of goods, in community of work; it is a commune, a true living together in unity and harmony.

The first or highest grade of unity exists when the Spirit of God's heart is united with the spirits of the believing Church; when the spirits of men become one with God's Spirit of perfect unity and unanimity.

The second grade of unity is the unity of heart of all those who belong to the believing Church, attuned to one another, pulsating and feeling in unison. In the individual this second grade of unity is expressed when the Holy Spirit, who

Marriage and the State

rules in man's heart, fills and dominates man's soul as well with all the perceptions and powers of its emotions. When this happens in a community of believing and loving people, then the movement of common joy binding heart to heart occurs between people.

The third grade of unity belongs to the material world. In the church-community it is expressed in two areas of life. It first becomes realized in all matter and work. The incarnation of Christ takes place in the united body of His community of work and goods, in the uniting of strength. And finally, this penetration of matter by the unity of spirit and soul is expressed by the physical and emotional union in the founding of community between two people. Just as the earth brings its blessing and brings forth its fruit again and again with the help of the rain and the sun, the powers of the earth and the natural order, so it is in the family. The family is given so that children may be born and raised through the uniting of bodies in community of spirit and soul.

Marriage, belonging to the third grade of unity in matter, may then seem to be lowly and of small value, for it unites the material and physical powers of human beings. But this apparent lowliness of marriage, which often enough is regarded and treated with disdain, is in truth and in the deepest sense the highest possible exaltation of matter and of mankind. God's Spirit did not hesitate to use the family bond of brothers and sisters as an example of the bond of body and soul between members of the Church. Nor does God hesitate to take the physical union of human beings as an example and image of His highest will and of the task He has intended for mankind and the earth.

The prophets and apostles saw that just as God and His people are one, in the same way husband and wife are one with one another. The unity between God and His Church can best be understood through the example of the unity between man and wife. In order to emphasize this truth, the prophet Hosea was given the tremendous mission of showing by his own destiny how far astray God's own people had gone, so that God could bring them back to make them His bride. The adultery of the people does not mean a sexual sin; it means that they left the spiritual covenant of faith for the false bond with idols, false teachings, and confusion. Through the

Marriage and the State 51

shaking example of his own fate in marriage, Hosea showed that just as compassion and love were shown to his wife, so too God will show compassion and love to His people, and on a higher level.

In the Church which was given through Jesus Christ and His Holy Spirit this recognition becomes broader and deeper. Again the word adultery is used and again it refers not to sexual transgression, but to the injury of the highest unity between God and His Church. Here again it is said: You adulterers, do you not know that the friendship of the world is hostility to God? You cannot serve two masters. No one can be the world's friend and God's friend at the same time. You cannot have mammon, money, and injustice for your spouse and at the same time make God and His love and justice your husband and lord. Only one of the two is possible. Either you submit to the King of God's kingdom, trusting in His loving guidance, or you submit to the powers of the violent sword and the executioner's axe and become their slave.

Here, however, is the gospel of truth: You shall no longer be the servants of men, nor shall you any longer let yourselves be swayed back and forth by different opinions. You must and shall be united with the Spirit of God alone, in the freeing, loving strength of Jesus Christ. Then you will also find true unity, love, and joy in marriage. Apostolic Christianity foresaw what the prophets of the Old Testament had already foreseen; to renounce the usual ways of the world would mean persecution. Because of this, all those who unreservedly enter into the covenant of unity with God give themselves up to the need and pain of being misunderstood, misinterpreted, and persecuted. Readiness to go into need and death is a part of the way of faithfulness and unity in the spirit of mission. For things will go so far that many will think they are doing God a service when they subdue and stamp out these "false men of God."

From all this it becomes clear what place marriage occupies within the people of God and within the Church. In the order of God's people it has the third place.

The first grade of unity is the complete unity of spirit between God and the Church. Everything must be sacrificed for this unity of spirit. The second grade of unity is the unity of souls amongst all in the community of believers. For this second grade, the third grade of family unity must be sacrificed whenever necessary. The third grade is by no means despised or humiliated by the two greater unities; rather, the destiny of the third grade is to make the first and second grades understandable to those who otherwise have no way to approach them. It does this through its love and faithfulness, its clear and indestructible unity. The third grade of family unity is embedded in the unity of the Church and the unity of the Spirit, so that even the dullest people can thereby recognize the spirit of unity that is revealed there.

Marriage, as the third grade of unity, is a part of the material reality of creation; it is a part of nature, which also exists without the gospel of Jesus Christ and without the Spirit. Therefore we must come to an understanding with the government in regard to this aspect of marriage. For us, marriage is not dependent on the government. But in regard to this third grade of unity we have to recognize the order of the state that is set over us. We welcome the fact that this order has provided for public notification, thereby relieving us of much that we would otherwise have to do ourselves. For marriage is a public fact, and therefore a public announcement of it is the state's concern.

We submit to the order of the state as long as this order is not in opposition to the first order, the unity of the Spirit, and the second order, the unity of hearts, in the Church. We completely recognize the order of the state as a necessity for unredeemed mankind within the material order. As long as mankind has not found the highest unity in God's Spirit and the second grade of unity in the uniting of hearts, the nations need this imperfect government to care for their affairs in the material order. The calling of the church-community is to make decisions in all things concerning the unity of spirit and soul, to keep itself free from all deeds of violence by governments, and to carry out its communal life in work.

In order to bring the spiritual effects of the final unity in God's kingdom and in the Church of Jesus Christ into harmony with the existing order of governmental authority and its might, we must make a clear and clean decision in each individual situation. In this way we are able to conform where possible. But when there is a question of complying with the state in its use

Marriage and the State

of force and violence, we must refuse to do this and make the decision to obey God rather than men.

Thus we consider that it is fitting for our couple to go to the registry office and register their marriage; this has to be done. Through this order of the state the marriage is made known to the material world. The real marriage or wedding, however, does not take place through the power of the state. It can take place, be pronounced, and confirmed through the spiritual unity of the Church alone and by those empowered by the Church. Thus we stand with the family in the midst of this world, a world which is not yet penetrated by the spirit of full unity. We are in a hard fight against a hostile government which would like to enslave our souls and spirits with false teachings, a government which again today would like to oppress our hearts and which has nothing in common with the way of Jesus Christ.[1] We stand in the midst of this world as a fighting and persecuted group, persecuted for the sake of the cause of complete community of faith and unity of God's people. Let us always keep this persecution in mind and never forget

[1] Hitler's National Socialist government, 1933

that it is hard and heavy, but that it will yet lead to victory and to the final goal of peace. "Do not be led away by diverse and strange teachings; for it is well that the heart be strengthened by grace."[1] Today many diverse and strange teachings are trying to gain ground in so-called Christianity. All these teachings are strange insofar as they do not convey the pure teaching of Jesus Christ and His spirit of unity and justice, but seek coercion and suppression.

We also are thinking of the families of the young couple. We know well that as yet these families are not in a position to understand the task of the Spirit which is entrusted to us. We know, too, that they are largely on the side of the persecution. For our part we wish them peace. We have the certain hope that through this marriage and through the affirmation of our brotherly unity the spirit of peace and justice may move in and take the place of discord and injustice. We wish with all our hearts that the step we are taking today in the strength of the spirit of the Church will lead these families to a true and genuine peace and justice of God. May this founding of a new family, then, help the old

[1] Heb. 13 . 9

families to be gripped anew by the spirit of unity, of peace, and justice, by the one spirit of truth which allows no mixing with strange teachings.

We charge you, then, with the task of taking this step courageously. Tomorrow we can go on to the actual blessing of the kingdom of God and His Church.

This bond in the Church of the spirit of unity will be blessed. We shall ask God to pour out over you the powers of the future world and to give you the powers of His first creation and last creation in the kingdom of God. By virtue of the perfect unity of the Spirit, in the name of the Church, you shall be a true marriage for ever and always before God and men.

THE MYSTERY OF UNITY

IT IS IN the family that there is still preserved, out of the first creation and the old nature, the best of what God has implanted in men. Nevertheless, marriage and the family have a much deeper unity in the true community and Church than nature is able to give. What is the real nature of marriage, then? Marriage is the bond between two human beings which is so firmly sealed that the two become one; then there are no longer two, but actually one. For this reason the Brothers, to whom we in our church-community belong, always referred in their writings to the union of two in this most profound sense of the church-community or *Gemeinde*.

Is there not something still higher by which two may yet become one, something higher than the bond between man and woman? Is it not true that even in the case of one who remains single and never marries, there is a like mystery by

The Mystery of Unity

which two become one? It was not only one poet who said, "Two souls dwell within my breast." Every human being feels a division between body and spirit; not only between body and spirit but also between spirit and soul. Often what a man wills in his inmost religious spirit is different from what he wills in the inmost feelings of his soul.

The unity which is shown in marriage must be revealed in every individual as well. Man's spirit must be united with his soul and his body. Man's spirit is different from his soul. Man's spirit is the place where the voice of God speaks to him. Man's soul means his innermost feeling, which is affected by every bodily impulse and every influence from outside. Man's soul hovers between his spirit and his body. It is something intermediate between spirit and body, held more closely to the body than to the spirit; and so to many it seems completely impossible that spirit, soul, and body should ever be entirely one. We must not despise the body and soul, for both are created by God. Soul and body must come under God's hand. This takes place through man's spirit. The Spirit of God must bear witness in our spirit, in the human spirit. Then man's spirit shall rule his body and soul.

What is the place of the soul in the Church? Here we come to the same mystery of unity. We cannot simply say of fifty or a hundred persons that they become united through one soul influencing another. Our souls can be united in one purpose and one harmony and one rhythm only when the Spirit rules and unites these souls. We think it is very important that our hearts, our souls, and feelings continue in joy and love in a mutual relationship. We know, however, that this cannot happen at all without the Spirit; or more correctly put, it cannot remain steadfast without the Spirit.

The impulse of the soul is a very uncertain foundation. It can be something quite wonderful, and it can be something desperately unhappy. The interrelation of souls is something very uncertain in itself, but it gains certainty and firmness when the Spirit rules and penetrates the soul. Here we find that noblest unity between souls of which the writings of the Brothers speak; that is, the noblest unity that we human beings are able to attain.

The highest unity we experience in the Church is this: The Holy Spirit comes upon us, and the Holy Spirit penetrates and unites our hearts.

The Mystery of Unity

Through this our bodily powers, too, are given to the service of the Holy Spirit. This means that physical and material things, including the sphere of work, are shaped and given form according to the will of the Holy Spirit.

The middle or second unity consists of the unity of body, soul, and spirit in man; it is possible only through the grace of Christ. The highest unity is the complete unity of our souls brought together in and by the Holy Spirit. In this way matter and will are formed and shaped according to the will of the Spirit. For this reason the apostle Paul speaks of the Church as the organism, the Body of Christ.

By this ultimate unity we are to understand that the Holy Spirit, who comes to us in Christ from God, unites with the spirits of the believers. This is the only way our hearts can be united, the only way we can shape material things according to the Spirit's will. All this is the mystery of marriage. Paul says in one of the most important chapters he has written on marriage:[1] I speak of the mystery of Christ and His Church.

This is a wonderful thing. It is a profound mystery and there are few who comprehend it.

[1] see Eph. 5

The one God unites with His one people; the one Christ unites with His one Church, His bride; the one Holy Spirit joins with the united spirit of the one Church, with the united spirits of believing men. To begin with, two things stand facing each other which then become completely one. For this reason the image of the Church is the image of marriage. Two become one, thus they are no longer two. This is the mystery.

In God himself we see something completely beyond our reach, something which we can never attain. There, not only two are one but three are one: the Father, the Son, and the Holy Spirit. These three are so completely one that no one of them is without the other. We do not need to philosophize or theologize about the meaning of the three in one. We need only to comprehend the one mystery: Where God truly is, there are Christ and the Holy Spirit. Where the Holy Spirit comes down to us, God the Creator and Christ come down to us, for the Holy Spirit brings all God and all Christ down to us. The apostle could therefore say outright: God is Spirit.

This is the greatest mystery. The mystery of unity is the mystery of God. The mystery of unity is the mystery of God's kingdom. The

The Mystery of Unity

mystery of unity is the mystery of the Church. The mystery of unity is the mystery of Christian marriage. It is a deep mystery, but very simple for those who can grasp it.

FAITH AND MARRIAGE

WHEN our couples marry, they answer several questions. These questions point to the relationship between unity of the Church and unity in marriage.

Is the unity of the Church more important to you than anything else? Is the unity of the Holy Spirit more important to you than anything else? Is the highest unity that God's Spirit can have with man's spirit, then, more important to you than anything else? And consequently, is the unity between heart and heart in the whole Church more important to you than the unity between only two? Or, to ask the question in a very practical form: Is unity of faith more important to you than emotional unity, for your marriage?

Is it clear to you, then, that your marriage is not based on a purely human mutual attraction, but rather that unity in your marriage depends

Faith and Marriage

on the unity of the whole Church? If so, it will be clear to you that through this unity, of which your marriage is a part, your marriage is truly indissoluble. Or in other words, just *because* the smaller unity between you two is subordinated to the greater unity of Christ's Church, the unity between you is steadfast. This is something very remarkable to the nonbeliever. He would think that the more independently a marriage unity is built upon the natural unity of two the firmer it is. That is an error. Nothing is firm but the eternal. Everything else is uncertain. Only when we make our marriage bond part of the eternal order is it a firm bond.

Thus we come to a surprising paradox. We put the question: if one of you were to be unfaithful to the Church, would the other one then remain in the Church and not follow the unfaithful one? It is clear to us that just this radical question constitutes the deepest security of a marriage bond founded in the eternal order. It places each of the marriage partners completely into the unity of the spirit of the Church, and in doing so, into unconditional faithfulness to one another. Merely to look at modern marriages attests to this truth. Marriages that are built purely on mutual inclination and attraction so often end in divorce nowadays, more so than in previous centuries. In the many years of the Hutterian church-communities, for instance, no marriage has ever been divorced, and the faithfulness and unity of marriages have been kept with joy in these four hundred years of community life.

The conclusion to be drawn from this whole concept of marriage is that unity of faith is the only possible basis for the whole of life, and this includes marriage. From this we see clearly that in marriage the most important thing is not the marriage as such, but the unity of God's kingdom in Christ, in His Holy Spirit. We would not recognize a marriage in which anything else had the most important place. It is just as Jesus says, "Strive first for the kingdom of God and His justice, and everything else shall be given to you"[1] — for the married or the unmarried. Marriage is only one example from actual life; the same is true of everything else. Marriage belongs to life in God and His Church.

[1] Matt. 6.33

CONSCIENCE AND RESPONSIBILITY

TODAY there is a widely accepted concept of family life, a concept which has strayed from the direction in which the family's responsibility and task are in keeping with God's creative will. The mutual relationships of a great number of young people, as well as those of their parents, are lacking the sense of responsibility which carries life and yet lays the whole of life in the hands of the faithful and uniting Spirit.

The destruction of the deepest emotional need for faithfulness does not disturb the consciences of countless people today; nor does the prevention and annihilation of the tiny beings who want to be called to life disturb the consciences of countless people. Little souls wait in vain to be called out of eternity. Living human souls wait in vain for the call of steadfast faithfulness. There seems to be an ever smaller number of people whose consciences protest clearly and definitely against the contempt for the creative Spirit, as well as against every frustration of the longing for unity, faithfulness, and constancy.

Many teachers of ethics demand that sex life be purified, that marriage be built upon former purity and be kept pure. This is an unfair demand unless the true foundations for the fulfilment of such a high demand are clearly set forth. Without faith in the kingdom of God it is impossible to take up the fight against the massacre of the innocents at Bethlehem multiplied indefinitely in the murder of life waiting to come into being. The supposedly high culture of our time will continue to practice this murder constantly, as long as social disorder and injustice last. Infant murder cannot be fought so long as private and public life are allowed to remain as they are.

Private property, and the lie and injustice of social stratification must be fought realistically by demonstrating the feasibility and reality of a different kind of life. Only then can one demand purity in marriage and freedom from murder. Not even for families with the highest moral standards can one wish the large number of children intended by God's creative powers. Christian marriage cannot be demanded outside of a life founded on the kingdom of God and the Church of Jesus Christ.

Marriage is the sole fulfilment of the sexual conscience. The sexual conscience is only fulfilled in marriage, through the will to have children. Marriage is the image of the unity of God with His people. Marriage is the pattern of the rulership of the spirit of unity. Marriage is community of life and goods. Marriage symbolizes the dominance of spirit over soul and body. In all this, marriage is the image of the Church. The Church is its place. One can make this demand of marriage only where the Spirit brings material things into community through the unity of the Church and through inspired and united work. Only in the Church can marriage be fulfilled at the right time and given its true value.

The unique unity and purity of marriage which Jesus and His apostles showed, belongs not to the old nature, but to the order of the Church. Here brotherly justice allows the spirit of love to rule over all things. The unity and purity of marriage is not part of the old Adam. It can only be carried out in the new Church of the Spirit of Jesus Christ. It belongs to the kingdom of God. It is its symbol and sacrament.

THE BOND OF THE SPIRIT

As WE SPEAK about marriage we recall the German youth movement of the early twentieth century which conveyed a new feeling for union with nature, for the fellowship of men, and for the liberty of boys and girls to get acquainted with each other. There, something became living once more which had almost been forgotten. It is difficult to place oneself in the position of young people about the year 1900. The youth of that day were firmly rooted in middle-class conventions. Social custom, strict rules and regulations encased them in a suit of armor. Obviously people were afraid that without this armor the worst might happen at any moment. There was no association between boys and girls. Right down into the lower middle class there was a carefully thought out supervision which took special pains to see that young girls did not go out with young men.

The Bond of the Spirit

What was the chief thing recognized by the youth movement with regard to the mutual relationship of man and woman, of boy and girl? The main recognition arose from the fact that nature requires of us and gives us a feeling for the wholeness of life. Whoever is in living touch with nature—on a hill, on the water, on a great mountain—is at the same time united in a common bond with all those people who have the same experience. Most important for these young people was the experience that in the feeling of communion with nature they sensed the community of the group, of the hiking troop, or of the little band. In this feeling of community, young people experienced a fellowship of trust so free from sensual desire that to think immediately of engagement and marriage or of other emotional relationships would have been grotesque.

The following thesis was accepted in the youth movement: if we are drawn into a real experience of fellowship, our human souls will be so united that when boys and girls do meet we need not expect an emotionally binding relationship. On the contrary, we can hike, dance, sing, talk, and work together without assuming that emotional or sexual relationships must arise.

Part of the youth movement went a little further. As the movement grew a little older, the purely negative attitude to marriage and to erotic relationships between man and woman had to make way for a more mature attitude. It was like this: one experienced an emotional, romantic feeling for nature and for community, a feeling of union with nature, and a feeling of human solidarity and comradeship. This inner experience of fellowship and of nature produced a common obligation for a group of young people to live together, at least for a limited time, for the purpose of a common fight against a degenerate and soulless social order.

Thus it came about that the relationships between boys and girls came under the influence of emotional ties. In this part of the youth movement, whose first founders were already twenty-five to twenty-eight years old, it was no longer expected that one should keep free of erotic experiences, but it was expected that physical union should and could come only from emotional oneness. Oneness of two souls was the premise. People could only come to a physical union when they had found each other emotionally; when on the emotional plane they had won

The Bond of the Spirit

a love and reverent appreciation for each other; when something great and beautiful was revealed to them in this oneness of souls.

Now I want to try to explain the attitude of the church-community to these questions. In the youth movement the emotional experience of nature and the feeling of community in the fellowship of the road were deemed fundamental to the soul's need of love. In the Church, however, it is the spirit of profound and ultimate community that is the deepest source of all experiences of life. Put more strongly: the youth movement rejected physical union without emotional unity as an abuse unworthy of man, and demanded the unity of souls of two people as essential for marriage. The church-community goes further and says: real unity of souls is absolute and complete only when it proceeds from the unity of the spirit of the Church.

We must first become one in the spirit of faith, in the spirit of uniting love, in the complete unity of God. Then we will be able to experience an emotional harmony which kindles a fire of human sympathy. In this human sympathy we shall experience something similar to that which was felt in the youth movement. We shall have a warm feeling for nature and for what God has given us in the first creation. We shall have great joy in one another every time we meet and speak and shake hands. We shall have great understanding for the varied emotions which sway our circle of men and women. But in the Church of unity all this is confirmed and guided by the Spirit.

The purification of emotional relationships by the Spirit is of a higher order than the purification of the love life by emotional unity. This is going a step further, for the unity of the Church in the Holy Spirit is greater than an organic unity of emotionally inspired bodies and greater than all other experiences. We need not fear, however, that the emotional atmosphere is disregarded in the Church. We can definitely expect the emotions uniting people to produce a relationship similar to that in the youth movement, only more constant and definite. All members of the common table and common household are united by a sense of fellowship which is very similar to that of the youth movement. We think of this life and activity when we read the words, "In God we live and move and have our being."[1]

[1] Acts 17 . 28

The Bond of the Spirit

Because we live in God, a thread of living relationships and loving mutual interest makes its way among us all, a thread that can never be broken so long as the life-giving Spirit continues to spin it anew.

Only on the basis of these two facts, unity in the Spirit and unity of souls, can marriage be given. It does not necessarily follow that it should be given. There may be people among us who are so filled with love to all men, to the community household, to guests, and to other people, that they feel no need as a man to win a girl or as a girl to belong to a husband. There are people who are so taken up by joy in all men that they have no energy left for an individual relationship to an individual human being. Paul saw this as a special gift. But boys and girls, men and women, because they have a task to preserve the human race, will be led ever anew to strong mutual relationships and through these to physical union. And this physical union can be joyful and meaningful only when it is born of unity of spirit and of soul.

The youth movement could find no clear attitude to the problem of marriage. Their experience was one of nature, an experience of union with nature and union of human beings with one another. On this basis of the purely natural creation there is no clear order for marriage. One cannot say it follows from the story of creation that it is imperative *one* man should have *one* wife. There is no reason to be found in the world of nature or in history for one definite order of marriage. Even where emotional unity is required and all merely physical attachments are rejected as unworthy, still Christian marriage does not result.

Christian marriage is intended by God to have more than historical significance. It has an immanent and a transcendent significance. Christian marriage is not based on the evidence of natural conditions in woods, fields, and pastures and among different peoples; nor is it based on what has become custom in the course of centuries. That is not possible.

Christian marriage can have its origin only in the other world. Its significance is purely religious. This religious significance is based on the comparison of unities; as the one God has His one people, as the one Christ has the one Church, so one man has his one wife; as the one Spirit unites with the inspired unity of the gathered

The Bond of the Spirit

Church, even so one man unites with his one wife.

The New Testament and the early Christians represent that of all the possibilities for founding a family, monogamous marriage is the highest and most worthy basis. This religious basis leads to a fulfilment not given by any other ordering of these matters. One must consider that all this only applies to those people who come to physical union through an emotional relationship based on the Spirit alone. It cannot be applied to civil law marriage. There it does not come into question. This matter is clearly a concern of the Church.

We find exactly the same is true in the question of marriage as in the use of force and in other questions of governmental authority. We cannot ask the state or any individual who is striving for authority in the state to use no arms. These things are imperative in order to suppress evil and to protect good, to fight injustice and support justice. But we must confess that the Church of Christ may under no conditions use the sword. In other words, if anyone uses the sword he may have acted rightly from the point of view of the state, but with this act he cuts himself off from the atmosphere of the kingdom of Christ. He has surrendered to the atmosphere of might and political power. It is a matter of deciding whether we want and are able to take our stand on the side of the communal life experience, or whether we want to remain in the natural sphere of human probabilities. In the latter case we can at best attain the attitude of the youth movement which was beyond doubt a great improvement upon the mire of the cities.

We must ask our guests to look deeply into this Christian basis, now that the marriage of our Kurt and Marianne is about to take place. Some may say this is truly an unnatural affair. That is so. Yet it must be understood that the natural element of the creation is included in this marriage of the Spirit. The early Christians were in no way hostile to the inclusion of the natural element of creation in marriage. They in no way defamed, debased, or disparaged the sexual life; on the contrary, they placed it under the guidance of the Spirit. On the natural plane, marriage guided by Christ becomes very natural. It does not condone the prevention of children, but would have a revulsion, a feeling of

The Bond of the Spirit

sin and perdition if it should seek to avoid giving birth to children. In such a marriage there will be as many children as possible, to the limits of health.

The objection of a guest, who considered the latter an economic question, was answered by Eberhard Arnold as follows:

Communities of life similar to ours should be founded and carried on. The spirit of the Church and the inner life of the Church are the premise. Then the economic possibility must be placed where it belongs. That is to say, the sexual question cannot be cut off from all the other questions of life. We feel that the regulating of economic conditions must arise from the spirit of the Church. The economic conditions cannot be separated from the social conditions. There must be a place where every child is regarded and accepted as a gift of God.

RESPONSIBILITY, DESIRE, AND LOVE

TODAY, as never before, it is high time to declare: away with the lies and the meaningless, empty words about sex, away with sexual hate and superstition! Together with all young people who are urged as we are by this concern, we cannot be silent. Together we must strive for clarity and truth in a life question that goes deeper than any other.

In this area of life, more than in any other, courage for truthfulness is the pressing need. We must be ready to let ourselves be judged so that within us and around us a place may be made for new and pure growth. It is not a matter of any one person being better than any other, but a matter of an awareness of a deep inward solidarity, of equality in the struggle, in all the pain and guilt. In no other area of life do truthfulness and responsibility more strongly forbid

Responsibility, Desire, and Love

passing on or allowing to go unopposed whatever is untrue or irresponsible, whatever is unclear and not fought through, whatever is not good and still carries poison within it, whatever is impure and enlarges the stain on the conscience, whatever is unfaithful and injures the responsibility of trust.

For this very reason, those who feel any responsibility find it infinitely difficult to speak up. Nothing but pure clarity, which we do not have, can stop the torment of uncertainty and indecision. Any word spoken in this sensitive area has an enormous effect. Whoever feels that silence and waiting are the greater wrongs must dare to speak out for purity and freedom just as clearly and definitely as it has been revealed to him.

In its actual effect upon the weak, the noblest but undecided struggle can be just as devastating and destructive as the lowest filthiness. Already during the early times of the art of printing, Agrippa of Nettesheim in *The Vanity and Uncertainty of the Sciences* said that no guns are as powerful in capturing a castle as the reading of poetry is in conquering and overcoming chastity and modesty. He names artists as the most useful instruments of matchmaking. Second only to the influence of literature he mentions the influence of persuasion and the arts in the service of seduction.

A great deal depends on the decision to seek one's own way with responsibility and truthfulness. But even more depends on the fact that everyone who is of the truth hears the voice of truth and gains his direction on the path upon which he will not slip away from life.

It is true that the law of love knows only one crime: the lie. There is but one sin: sacrilege against life. But is it an overcoming of sexual sin when one believes in sensual pleasure as one believes in a god who can destroy lies and deception? Up to now, anyone with vision has seen that nowhere has there been more perjury, more broken oaths, more spiritual murder than in the self-deceit of sensuality, than in the self-deceit of enjoyment derived merely from the senses. Most shocking of all is that again and again the ignoble conduct which deceives and breaks trust is afterwards represented as something quite different from what it actually was. By means of such untruthfulness we try to protect ourselves from the Furies of our consciences. We try our utmost to see the loved one not as base, but as

Responsibility, Desire, and Love

good as possible in every way. Yet anyone who, like Mme. de Stael, has tried out of love to carry this untruthfulness through to the end will feel that she was right in saying, "A dagger thrust is punished by law, and the wounding of a feeling heart is the subject of a joke; it would be better to suffer the dagger thrust."

The wounding of soul and spirit by the lack of responsibility in love is sin; its effect is more murderous than the killing of the body. Responsibility for oneself, for one's fellow men, and for the effect upon all men, will never tolerate physical harmony being seen as something separate from the spiritual, and from the unity of conscience in the spirit.

Euripides asked, "But what is that which men call love? It is the most wonderful thing, my daughter, and the bitterest!" We must be aware of this tension and carry it reverently through all our speaking and living; only then will the truth be able to reach us. Otherwise, in all of our striving for truthfulness, responsibility, and purity the judgment of Schopenhauer will apply to us, "In the struggle with this passion, there is no motive which is so strong that it can be certain of victory."

Any separated, isolated form of pleasure in one's own body, such as the vice of masturbation, is disastrous. A child should regard it as his duty to resist this inclination because there is more at stake here than health and bodily harm. If in the past there has been a good deal of exaggeration in this direction then more clarity is needed now. The calamity consists not in the danger of physical disease, not in the consequences, but in the spiritual and emotional source of such an act.

This vice of the body has its origin in the fantasy of the physical, emotional, and spiritual life. It is far removed from the possibility of true community which can come only from the unity of spirit through the emotional into the physical. Something happens here which is separated from the spirit, something which defiles the thought of community, which degrades every person in his own eyes. Impure and sordid elements lie in the imagination which, separated from the spirit, tries to steal something for itself for which the moral obligation, moral justification and the responsible power of the spirit are lacking.

Thus it is a matter of spiritual purity reflected

Responsibility, Desire, and Love

in physical purity. The freeing and cleansing of the imagination can penetrate only in the realm of the soul and only there bring about new physical purity and freedom, even when purity and freedom have been lost for a long time.

Purity is reverence for the meaning of love. The unveiling of the body's secrets and of the mysteries of procreation and birth before many people is a lack of reverence, a betrayal of what is sacred and will remain sacred only if kept for the one great experience of two. The temple is desecrated when it has become a public place accessible to every profane look. The more highly one thinks of the emotional and physical love life the more respect and reverence are needed not to betray it. This reverence will be felt strongly only if people are aware of the tremendous contrasts connected with love: the lowest degradation and the rarest height of human life, the filthiest breath of plague and the purest air of the spirit.

We owe to love the finest productions of art in poetry and music and painting, as well as the entire cycle of nature and life. We recognize in love the basis of civilization and the family, of the peoples, and of the whole development of mankind. And at the same time we see the consuming flame that drives countless unhappy people into ruin and crime.

Love is either abundance of life, of generation, birth, and creation; sacrifice and redemption — life itself; or else what is called love is the poisoning and killing of life; it is sin the weapon of death. Vice is death.

Moralism has nothing to say to these questions. Civil codes and social traditions cannot be authoritative in regard to the basic forces of life. One needs only to think of the bondage and slavery of the marriage duty under the German Civil Code against which the women's ethical movement rightly fought. Instead of the duty of civil law they wanted marriage firmly founded on faithfulness, cleansed of mammonism and serfdom. The point is not to defend something old or to make a new attack; what is at stake is not the different forms of church or civil marriage. Everything depends on achieving a higher, deeper morality through the deepening and fulfilment of its substance.

Sensuality when repressed or suppressed by moral compulsion, convention, or legal control throws itself into ever new channels of untruthfulness or perverse aberrations. We should strive neither for the monastic ideal nor for the libertine ideal. Sexual repression, like sexual subjection, begets equal oppression and falsity in all other areas of life as well. To be cold and without desire can never be considered a virtue.

An intellectual consideration, an intention of the will, a dogmatic or social tradition can never be the decisive factor between life and death. But neither can sacrilege against life, the wounding and destruction of life's innermost and holiest values, the forsaking and discarding of entrusted and trusting life, appear as an improvement of the new life over the old. It is not true that "Whoever has never exchanged forbidden kisses, never been intoxicated with sinful love ... has forgotten how to live!" That which is called sin by the creator of life, that which is disclosed as sinful by the bringer of life upon the earth is always one thing: sacrilege against the soul, the destruction of life in body and soul.

Certainly we know that other influences of death have flowed as undercurrents into institutional Christianity. Legalistic morality and Neoplatonic introspection have caused an estrangement from life. Nietzsche's saying cuts two ways, "Christianity has given Eros poison to drink.

He did not die of it, but degenerated to a vice." This is a judgment on a corrupted Christianity's enmity to the body, but it also opens up the question of why Eros could and had to succumb to this poison. Was Eros really poisoned only by Christianity? Of course this is not the case.

Eros has no exceptional position in life. The sexual life, like everything else, is subject to the laws of the soul and the spirit. When people, who in other respects seem to show courage and strength of conscience, are weak in this area of responsibility and are miserably defeated, this fact throws a harshly illuminating light on the total picture of their lives. Impurity never pollutes us from without, nor can it ever be outwardly wiped away at will. It breaks out of the innermost state of the spirit like an infected sore from the poisoning of the whole bloodstream, and leaves behind indelible traces in the character, a rent in the soul, a loss in the sense of responsibility for people, corruption of the conscience, death.

It is clearly evident that there can be no desire that is amoral, that is without moral responsibility. If desire were a narcosis, an intoxication in the sense of a loss of awareness,

Responsibility, Desire, and Love 89

in the sense of an elimination of responsibility, then it would indeed be a negation of the spirit which makes the man. Desire would then be the deepest degradation, never the highest blessing. Then perfection would really be lack of desire. Then the highest spirituality would, in fact, mean the greatest possible denial and overcoming of every natural wish. But that cannot be. Certainly no desire can degrade man more easily than the will to conception and birth. Yet every desire has in it something from God, otherwise it would no longer be living. Death alone is the ultimate enemy of divine life.

It is clearly seen that every desire becomes more brutish and low the more it is debased for the satisfaction of a refined lust, of a naked sensuality or debauchery, when gratification is used as the meaning and purpose of desire. But what does this mean: sexuality without love is the desecration of the mystery which fills the universe, the mystery of community between God, man, and nature? Is it not quite wrong to say that out of the storms of love the most unconscious sexuality shall emerge as the purest? It is true that the desire of the old life finds its mysterious consecration in the new life of a child.

But this consecration is the sanctification of the conscious responsibility of both loving persons for the future child. It is the sanctification of a responsibility that is enduring, lasting, never to be dissolved or given up.

Abstinence and activity only become good or bad according to their manner and object; just because of this it is necessary to be as clear as possible about the content and nature of the love life, whether it is abstaining or active. It is said that the sensual life of man deserves the same respect and sympathy as man himself. Yes, that is so. But the sensual is an area which reveals, more than almost any other area, what a person really is. If in this respect his actions toward his fellow men and toward himself are not good, then self-respect and sympathy for just what is most essential in man must be called into question.

"The mother of intemperance is not joy, but joylessness!" Sensual intemperance is not the human as created by God, but the all-too-human which is of the devil because it is inhuman, demonic. Gaining true life and learning to rejoice are the best ways to unlearn doing harm and thinking up injury to others. Then the stirring of the sensual emotions does not need to be rejected and struggled against, for then desire is at the service of a higher life and a better future. Then faith becomes decisive in the love life itself, and hope gives direction to the future. "Marriage: this is what I call the will of two to create a oneness which is more than those who created it. I call marriage reverence for one another as for those who have this will."[1]

It needs to be said clearly that faithfulness is the only attitude which is in keeping with the character of true love. There is but one unity and freedom in the love life, and that is faithfulness. It is the only attitude which corresponds to a sense of responsibility for one's own life and for the soul entrusted to one. Unfaithfulness is irresponsibility; it is lying, deathly wounding of the soul; it is sin against the soul, sacrilege against life. Faithfulness shows that the joy of love springs forth from permanent and ever new sources.

To say that love is nothing but an episode in a man's life is true only of a superficial relationship, a relationship of physical attraction which lacks the deeper communion of souls and is far

[1] Nietzsche, *Thus Spake Zarathustra*

removed from the spirit. Mutual love springing from a common spiritual content and from the harmony of emotions demands increasing mutual support. Such love can never end because it originates in the eternal Spirit and is independent of physical and emotional states.

Goethe distinguishes between the first outpouring of young love and the longing for marriage, home, and children of one's own; and distinguishes these from the emotionally mature love of full spiritual development. True marriage, then, would be that rare happiness which consists of the oneness of two originating in the spirit for the sake of the inner life of the family, the unity of two souls that reaches into every outpouring of love.

In this area it is clear how far removed from the physical appetites found on the city streets are the trust and the longing of love in the youth movement. All those who were in any way gripped by the youth movement confessed in common with Giordano Bruno, "In truth it is a sign of a base and vulgar disposition to direct one's whole aim and endeavor toward the merely physical beauty of a woman." It cannot be disputed that there is an inner and physical

Responsibility, Desire, and Love 93

state during which everything in us dies; in our spirit, in our heart, in our mind; duty, past, future. But Giordano Bruno shows himself to be a true champion of freedom and of the future life, for he recognizes clearly, "Love opens up paradise. Love is not blind, as many say. And love does not make everyone blind, but only those who are ignoble by nature. They are the ones who know only the bastard sister of love, inconstant sensual desire. True love illuminates, clears, and keeps the mind and spirit alert, and creates wonderful powers in those who are worthy of it . . . With the primeval stirring of the elements, quick as thought love penetrates every power far beyond its sphere and effect."

Where would soul and spirit be if the peace of perfection were seen to be in the physical? Can we still try to depict the landscape of the body impressionistically without the soul of the landscape, without the Spirit of God over the depths? Happiness of the senses does not bring peace of soul. Certainly it is not a matter of choosing between sensual enjoyment and peace of soul. It is a matter of the spirit which can bring peace of soul into the happiness of the senses. Spirit cannot be amoral; spirit is not irresponsible unawareness. Spirit is the holy power of conscious love which ennobles, completes, develops, and activates all powers. Only the penetration and deepening of the spirit, never physical desire, can satisfy the longing to be possessed with all one's soul, the longing that grows with sacrifice.

We all know that pleasure by itself kills. The separation of the soul from the senses is what truly debases. Nothing can be built up except upon relationships of the soul. On this we are agreed. But communion of souls can exist only in the coequal, enduring, ever deepening mutual trust built upon unity of spirit.

We want to leave behind us the degraded level of life in which the instinct of the flesh rules. We do not want to climb the false ladder of legalistic, moralistic churchdom. On the other hand, the path of unconscious ruling by the emotions and feelings follows the will-o'-the-wisp into the swamp. Love that is only emotional must rock like a boat on the sea. Such love cannot achieve anything eternal; it cannot achieve marriage whether it goes by the name of marriage, or liaison, or any other name.

The spirit of true love which is truth, wisdom, excellence, and self-control was already anticipated in pagan times. With Jesus the new possibility of being immersed in the Spirit has come to life. The instinct of the Holy Spirit comes into men's lives, stronger than the desires of the flesh, more substantial than any moral law. Being filled with this Spirit which Christ brings does not mean mental unawareness, but the opposite. It means that feeling and thought, joy and clear vision press forward to decision and determination of the moral will. In the doing of God's will, in the recognizing of Christ's will, the power of love of His Spirit is revealed. Spirit of Christ, Holy Spirit, leads to the doing of God's will and thus to faith in Christ and His future.

This Spirit from God seeks our spirit. Man is more than body and soul, more than animal. Man is spirit. Intellect and reason are not the whole of man's being. <u>The deepest in man is his consciousness of God, his feeling for the universe, his expectation of future unity in all things, the image of God in his longing for the All-One.</u>

We are so created by nature that our instincts are meant to come under the guidance of the spirit and to be healed should they grow diseased or degenerate. Man can govern his desires, like the members of his body, by the spirit. He should not yield himself without control to the magnetic forces of the blood. Even his subconscious is under the leadership and guidance of his spirit to the extent that man becomes man.

The mutual relationship between spirit and body indicates that there is nothing of the body for which man is not in some way morally responsible. It also points out that neglect and spoiling of the body and its nerves not only brings about physical slackness, but actually saps power from the spirit so that its stimuli and warnings no longer flow as in healthier times. Therefore the ethics of the body is an essential condition for a high spirituality, whether one thinks of gymnastics or of will power directed toward physical ends. Self-seeking, effeminacy, and untruthful self-indulgence are the evil sources of impure thoughts and wishes. This tendency to softness and spoiling must be opposed; then the power of resistance, also to specific sexual temptations, will of itself be stronger. Thus there is nothing physical which does not have its source and cause in the soul and ultimately in the spirit.

Only the unconditional love which is a gift of the Spirit creates marriage ever anew, marriage which can never be dissolved or destroyed. Only

Responsibility, Desire, and Love

infinite life is capable of infinite action, boundless fulfilment, and infinite pain. Love which is found in this way feels touched by the forces and the essence of the universe; it knows itself to be one with the powers which shape the future of humanity, the powers whose influence extends over tremendous spaces in distance and time, reaching infinitely further than we are able to reckon in thousands of years.

Here we are confronted with the question of God, insofar as the question can be understood by man. What distinguishes man from animal is the longing for unity of body and spirit, the sensing of the Spirit as the great eternal connection of all living things in love. Anyone who goes no further than this in his questioning and in his inner openness may doubt whether this eternal Spirit of infinity has consciousness, and he may thus consider the highest in his love of mankind to be unconscious. Yet anyone should be disconcerted by what led the "atheist" Voltaire to express in Lord Rochester's confession, "in a land of atheists, love would lead to the worship of God."

Jesus, through the men He sent into the world, carried the witness of His life and of His love-death over the earth. God is love. God is strength. God is Spirit. "As the Father has sent me, so I send you."[1] In Him the love of God appeared in a purity and clarity which no longer had anything to do with the physical sources of human powers of love. Thus He was able to intimate that there can be people who, deemed worthy of a special task of God's love, are released or absolved from physical love for the sake of the future world order based on love. In Jesus it is shown that the love which is from God and is poured out on men in His Spirit is not a sublimation of human desire. Rather, here it is revealed that the pure love which is in Christ has nothing to do with the emphasis on man and the emphasis on self which betray the core of death in even the most exalted human love.

It is clear that only from God, who alone holds everything in His hand, can we expect the answer. He gave examples of self-mastery to mankind. He has sent men of character who lived in life-affirming asceticism, without whose living example we could not hold out in this tremendous struggle. Such asceticism does not despise nature

[1] John 20 . 21

Responsibility, Desire, and Love

and the body. On the contrary, it points to a deep reverence for natural life, subordinating natural life to the unconditional rulership of the higher life of the spirit.

Freedom from possessive desire must be lived out as the freedom of outpouring love, as freedom of the all-embracing Spirit. Poverty and chastity shall be a living example to us, a sublime possibility of the highest will of love. Free-willingness and grace alone will lead to this way of obedience and faith; for it is God's Spirit who claims such obedience. On this way mere outward order is contrasted with the higher life. The higher life alone is capable of giving an inner direction to the practical everyday life of all men; for it springs not from rigidly exacting law but from bountiful grace. Marriage and career, society and state are not threatened by this living asceticism; instead, everybody is challenged to take up the crucial struggle within, which wills and ventures the victory of the spirit over material things everywhere, again and again.

Kant was obviously wrong in recognizing only cold duty and sensual inclination. The living soul knows another desire, one that strives for everlasting perfection, a desire quite different from the sensual driving force of a love life which is directed only to physical satisfaction and the feeling of the moment. It is an urge of the liberating spirit which is something completely different from moralistic compulsion. In man there is a sacred urge which in truth wants love, which always has in view the whole of life and everlasting perfection, rather than the momentary condition alone.

Such intense heightening of man's living activity opposes all possession, including the possession of love, whereas sensual desire and legal order have to be concerned with lust and possession. The spiritual urge seeks the ultimate, true value of life, the mystery of life, because it overcomes all other values. This deepest value of life lies in the indestructible community of spirits, in divine spiritual love which is free of sensuality and self-seeking. The urge to find this true value of life is the communal will of the spirit; it is the outpouring will to love; it is in God alone. It stands just as much opposed to the covetous sensual will as to moralistic law and order.

Man's love life will be healthy and happy in the deepest sense only when it is guided by this

Responsibility, Desire, and Love 101

ultimate evaluation of life. The rulership of the spirit means riches, for the spirit determines and guides and governs all living impressions in their manifold vitality. It does not destroy true values while overcoming false ones.

In practical life one can test the significance of this evaluation with every beloved person. Love begins with interest in the being of the person one loves, but love will rejoice in this being only if it recognizes in the beloved person the true worth of his or her innermost calling. Love's incentive is directed basically toward the perfecting of the beloved one, and always in the one sense: to recognize and enhance the worth of the beloved's life within life as a whole.

Every community which seeks this love is not built upon pleasure, but always and completely upon the importance of men's calling. Dedication, which is a part of love, will break through in men who are seized by this calling. The happiness of this pure love consists in putting aside one's sensual desires in the freedom which is given when the spirit rules one's life, when men's highest calling prevails.

Augustine shows us how today's questions have always been the concerns of mankind and its leading minds. His words about love, therefore, shall sound the closing note.

The love of man must be redeemed. "May its ardent fervor for the world become an ardent fervor for the Master of this world. Love, yes; but take care what it is you love. Love is the self of the soul, the hand of the soul. When it holds one thing, it cannot hold something else. If it is to hold what one gives it, it has to put down what it is holding. The one kind of love is turned toward community, the other is limited to the ego; the one looks to the good of all and thinks of the spiritual fellowship, the other tries to bring even the cause of fellowship under itself. The worth of a man is not to be assessed according to what he knows, but according to what he loves."

The love of God desires nothing. It only gives and sacrifices itself. Its only memorial is the cross.

THE PROMISE

IN A MEETING of the brotherhood, Eberhard Arnold asked Franz and Ilse to tell about the personal matters which are concerning them, and to talk with the brotherhood about them in an openhearted way.

Franz and Ilse affirm that they became engaged at the Eisenach colony with a view to their task for the colony. But since they have come to the Bruderhof and have dedicated themselves to the cause of God's kingdom, they feel more and more that this engagement is untruthful. They feel this way because they do not have the relationship of an engaged couple, but feel as brother and sister toward each other. For the sake of clarity in this matter, they both sought to talk with the word leader and suggested that their engagement be broken off.

EBERHARD: This is very difficult for us, for we can never do anything that could in any way be injurious to the pledged word.

HANS: I am thinking about the instance of someone who had given a promise, a commitment to the Werkhof-community near Zurich, a promise which seemed at one time to have been broken, but which was after all kept in a deeper and more essential way. This seems to me to be similar.

I think an engagement promise is something very important, and regardless of who knows about it, it is something very powerful. We ought to be shocked if such a promise were broken. Now we hear that the promise was given in a particular sense, in relation to the working together for a cause. But even if something was given in the sense of the working together of two people, I would like to express the hope that this promise might find its realization in the same powerful way that the promise given to the Werkhof-community found its realization. It is clear that even for married couples who come from outside, a completely new situation arises in the Church; marriage then takes on a completely different meaning than anywhere else.

EBERHARD: I, too, think that this very deep promise is the real cause of the difficulty. I understood you in this way: you would not have

The Promise

given this promise to each other if you had known what marriage really is, if the essence of marriage had been clear to you in a deep and substantial way, a way which is almost unknown outside. I mean the question of whether, at that time in Eisenach, you would have given each other this promise if you had recognized this deepest meaning and the infinitely deep nature of the married state.

ILSE: Perhaps we should have waited until it was given more clearly.

EBERHARD: You two aren't able to say anything now as to whether you are going in the direction of marriage?

ILSE: We must let ourselves be led in this.

EBERHARD: Could you say that it is impossible?

FRANZ: That is the feeling we have at the moment. Yet we have faith. If the church-community feels that something can really be given by the Spirit, that something can happen, then we also want to believe this.

EBERHARD: But that won't do. Franz, do you desire marriage? Do you request of me, as the servant of the Word, that you may be allowed to take the step of marriage?

FRANZ: No.

EBERHARD: Ilse, do you desire marriage?

ILSE: No. I first would like to grow into the life of the church-community.

EBERHARD: If you two do not desire marriage, then we cannot give you any advice at all. Nor can we say, "We wish you to become married." Suppose I should invite all those who wish and desire marriage to come and speak with me, then you two would not come?

FRANZ and ILSE: No.

EBERHARD: From this we see that we have no reason to say, "Through the leading of the Spirit in the Church, you should be joined in marriage." The leading of the Spirit in the Church has no wish at all to urge young people to marry as soon as possible. The Church has a different task.

When young people have the feeling — now, for the sake of true order, I should be married— the Church should see to it that the marriage can take place. From this you see, Franz, that I cannot do what you have just suggested. I cannot say, "I believe that you two are called to marriage and I wish that you might be married." For you yourselves do not desire marriage. You Franz, quite apart from Ilse, and you Ilse, quite apart from Franz, do not desire to be married!

The Promise

The difficulty between you lies somewhere else. It lies in the fact that you have given your word to one another, and we must honor and respect this word. That is why the question of the sense in which this word was given at that time was so important to me. Was it given for the sake of the Eisenach colony and for the standing together at the colony? Would this word have been given if the spiritual mystery of marriage, which is the third grade of unity, had been revealed to you? Did this engagement really mean marriage?

Hans said before, that marriage as you saw it had a particular task for the Eisenach colony and the hoped for community there; he wished for you two, that what you had intended by your marriage promise might be given to you now in a different way, as something which God alone can do. Is that quite clear? In this connection I said that the deepest mystery of marriage is almost unknown outside: Christ's mystery of marriage, which has been revealed to us here.

HANS: I mean, if there has been a marriage already outside, then it must be built anew from the ground up, on the basis of the Church. We should not be surprised, then, if promises which people have given to one another outside must be completely revised here: there has to be a thorough testing of the word once given. If afterward it is allowed to stand, then it is in fact the old word and yet again it is not; it is a word which has died and been given anew. True marriage, the completely Christian order of marriage, has been practically lost to the world.

Wherever people remain in the unmarried state within the Church, the very same thing which is the essence of true Christian marriage comes to expression, that is, the full dedication to unity and the complete surrender of self. And just because of this it is something quite unique when a marriage can be joined in the Church. The married as well as the unmarried place themselves completely in readiness for whatever is God's will. I fully agree that we have to say we do not know God's intention for these two. We wish that everything unclear might become quite clear. This happens through the spirit of the Church.

GEORG: The difficulty is that it does not seem clear to these two themselves how their promise was and is to be understood. Perhaps they should be given a time of waiting during which this question will be cleared up. That is what must first become clear. Both must grow more deeply in the understanding of what we mean by marriage in the Church. Then perhaps it will at last become clear how the promise made then is to be taken. A time of open waiting seems to me to be the appropriate thing, a time in which they decide neither one way nor the other.

EBERHARD: We are again at the decisive point. Now Franz and Ilse both express the feeling that they should release each other from this bond, without saying, however, that it is either possible or impossible that they might later be called to marriage. Do you believe that you must release each other from any claim upon one another? Or, do you first place a "no" against the old claim of your former "yes"?

To be sure, since you have in no way turned away from each other nor have any aversion for each other, there certainly remains the possibility that later God may lead you together through a special unity of spirit, which now seems and must seem quite unimaginable to you. In regard to your former promise and to your present attitude, do you feel that you must mutually release one another?

FRANZ and ILSE: Yes.

EBERHARD: Franz and Ilse have now mutually declared that they do not wish to be bound to their earlier promise and they feel freed and happy about this. That is a fact. We would, however, ask you not to make this known yet as a breaking of the engagement. If you were to write about this now it would seem as if you had come completely away from one another. I would suggest a period of half a year during which you are not considered an engaged couple either between yourselves or before the Church, but during which you write to each other in an open frame of mind about all current questions, especially about questions regarding the spirit of the Church. I would advise that for half a year you quietly persevere in this correspondence and consult together in writing. After this time of testing you will tell us the result. During this half year one of you should be on the Alm Bruderhof and the other on the Rhön Bruderhof. That would be a clear situation.

For when two people have been led as closely together as you were by this very earnest promise, you should not break off the dialogue suddenly, but at least continue it in writing. You don't need to write about questions regarding the en-

The Promise 111

gagement, but rather about questions of character, about God's kingdom, about spiritual questions of all kinds. You should wish for one another that through this mutual exchange your friendship is furthered. And we hope that after half a year both you and we can test and recognize what has become of your solemn and public promise and of your faithful relationship as true brother and sister. It follows from this, then, that Franz would go to the Alm Bruderhof immediately after the New Year.

EMMY: With every wedding something new becomes clear to all of us. Each time something quite new comes to us. The wonderful thing about the revelation connected with Christ is that again and again it is new, that it is never finished with. It is a mystery, something which lies in eternity: the marriage of Christ with His Church! There is still a great deal for the two to think about. We also know of a calling not to marry; that, too, is a mystery.

EBERHARD: The root of this whole confusion lies in the fact that in the Eisenach colony the essence of marriage was not clear. Even though you could not have known this at the time, there was complete unclarity about everything concerning engagement. This can happen now and then with young people, among us as well. I would like to ask all young people to listen with their inner ear, so that you do not find yourselves one day in a similar sad situation.

At the same time I must say that I know that this young couple have kept their betrothal in true modesty and purity, that they have nothing to reproach themselves with in their mutual relationship as an engaged couple. There is no question of any misconduct during the engagement, but simply a question of an inner development which came out of the ignorance of a false beginning. I mean ignorance in the sense of a lack of God's deepest revelation, in the sense of a lack of the Holy Spirit. Because of this, in the church-community the chasteness of attitude and inner restraint of young people is something of exceptional importance and meaning, so that no one may fall into such entanglements through a lack of the Spirit.

Within our confidential circle, then, it is absolutely clear that at the moment and in the near future you are not engaged, Franz and Ilse. But we advise a time of clarification and of waiting for you, during which you can let God's Spirit

The Promise

work freely again and in quite a different way, so that something quite new might happen between you. Even though you have mutually released each other and even though the Church must recognize the fact that neither of you desire marriage, yet the importance of this serious promise remains such a decisive factor that a half year of earnest testing and faithful correspondence is laid upon you, before a public announcement of your changed attitude can take place.

ENGAGEMENT

I FEEL IT IS important that our attitude as married people toward our young people is such that we rejoice when there are friendships between boys and girls, and when a mutual exchange in the common life comes about among them. We would fall into an entirely unnatural sphere if we no longer welcomed this relationship. First and foremost, I would like to ask everyone to always have a warm understanding for the need that young boys and girls in our midst have for this association of mutual trust. It is our wish that these young people may move about and have this comradeship in the sight of us all. They do not need to withdraw or remove themselves in any way; this comradeship can take place everywhere in the trust of the Church. There need be no timidity here, but a true freedom and openness.

It is all the more contrary to our way of life,

Engagement

then, when two young people go out and are absent late at night. This is contrary to the trust that we all have toward each other. Rather, this relationship between two young people should be under the protection of the whole Church's trust. We all know that when young people meet one another in the innermost and holiest things, their understanding and meeting in the emotions come from the Spirit.

An engagement is another matter. If there is a question of an approaching engagement, it is in keeping with our way of life that before the two young people commit themselves by any promise or arrangement, they speak with the word leader so that everything may take place according to God's will.

The truth revealed in the Hutterian marriage teachings is very simply expressed by Peter Rideman in his *Confession of Faith*. Everything that is true of marriage is also true of the time before marriage. It will come about through God's grace alone, that there can never be a purely erotic relationship among us, that there can be no love relationship which depends only on the magnetism of the nerves and the functions connected with this.

In a living church-community the point of departure will always be the Spirit of Jesus and His Church, which comes down to us. This means that the way to engagement is not prepared by mutual attraction or emotional relationships. Before entering into any physical-emotional relationship, a particular spiritual unity between two must be present. Only when the unity of two is pervaded by God's Holy Spirit, do we believe that they will be given the creative powers which come to new expression in the gospel of all creation. Only in the Holy Spirit can the bond of spirit, soul, and body, the procreation and birth of children, be given. That bodies are a living sacrifice upon the altar of God is a tremendous thing to believe. We are not worthy of it unless we believe that unity can be given.

This is the deeper meaning behind the fact that in a true church-community an engagement cannot be formed without the word leader and the brotherhood. It depends on the mystery of spiritual unity between two persons in all their uniqueness.

Engagement

Everything that happens belongs ultimately in the Church. This is not a matter of morals; it is a question of the special imparting of the Spirit, of inspiration, of unity, of the particular image of spiritual unity between two within the Church. In all these things the Holy Spirit must prevail.

THE THREE GRADES OF MARRIAGE

"MARRIAGE is a union of two, in which one taketh the other to care for and the second submitteth to obey the first, and thus through their agreement two become one, and are no longer two but one. But if this is to be done in a godly way they must come together not through their own action and choice, but in accordance with God's will and order, and therefore neither leave nor forsake the other but suffer both ill and good together all their days. Marriage is, however, in three grades or steps."[1]

First is the marriage of God to His people; the marriage of Christ to His Church; the marriage of God's Spirit to the spirit of man.

Second is the justice of God's people among themselves; the fellowship within the Church, the members of the Body of Christ forming a complete unity; the fellowship of spirit and soul.

[1] Rideman, "Concerning Marriage," *Confession of Faith*

The Three Grades of Marriage

Third is the unity between one man and one woman. This unity is not the first grade of unity; it is not unity proper. It is the last unity—visible, understandable, and recognizable by all.

Because marriage between man and woman is something that can be seen and grasped by everyone, it is an image, an outward sign of something invisible which is to become reality in the visible world. It is a sign pointing to the middle and highest grades of marriage. It points first to the fellowship of justice and brotherliness, the fellowship between God's Spirit and man's spirit. It points to the middle grade where everything in which we believe becomes visible. For as man is the head of woman, so the spirit is the head of the body, and God is the head of the spirit.

Thus marriage teaches us and leads us to God. When we regard and recognize marriage rightly, it teaches us to know God and hold fast to Him. If marriage is not regarded rightly, however, it leads men to death. There are not many who have truly recognized marriage, and therefore Paul says that a man does well not to touch a woman, lest in his ignorance he perish.

Man has the task of portraying the service of Christ. Woman has the task of portraying the dedication of the Church, of obeying her husband so that she may learn from him what the nature of the true God is. If she does not do this, she is forsaking her place in God's order. The man, for his part, has also received his place in God's order. He should have compassion for his wife, and in love and kindness care for her in material things and still more in spiritual things. The man should go before her in honesty and courage, so that through him she may become godly. For Christ's justice is to become manifest in man. If the man does not do these things but is negligent and irresponsible, he is forsaking the glory given him by God.

Both man and woman are given their tasks by God so that they may be led to recognize ever more deeply how the spirit must rule over the body and how God must rule over the spirit of man. The woman should follow the man just as the earthly body follows the heavenly, that is the spirit. She should follow, not from her fleshly or earthly will, but looking toward the Spirit and letting herself be ruled by the Spirit, looking toward Christ and letting herself be led and ruled by Him. When this happens in this way, man is kept close to God. Through the Spirit,

The Three Grades of Marriage

through the Christ and the God of justice, man is held close to God.

Marriage should not be undertaken in the will of the flesh — for the sake of beauty, youth, money, property, or anything of that kind. None of these things are of God. "As the angel said to Tobias, 'Hear what I say to thee and I shall show thee who they be over whom the devil hath dominion, namely, those who marry without regard to God in their heart, but only to satisfy the wantonness of the body, even as a mule or horse that knoweth no better; yea, over such hath the devil dominion.' "[1] Man, then, should not choose anything for himself through the willfulness of the flesh.

What God has joined together through the unity and unanimity of the Church must not be severed by man. The couple should be given to each other in public marriage, before the Church; the Church must testify that these two have been given to each other and that no man can sever them.

Marriage is an image of the unity between Christ and His Church. The image must have a resemblance and likeness to what it portrays.

[1] Rideman, "Concerning Marriage," *Confession of Faith*

So we should recognize that the third and lowest grade of unity, the unity between husband and wife, stands as a symbol for the middle grade.

The third and lowest grade of marriage, which we see so tangibly, points to the highest grade as well: the marriage between God and His people, between Christ and His Church, between the Spirit of God and the spirit of man.

Isaiah foretells the history of God's people in chapter 54:

> Sing, O barren one, who did not bear;
> break forth into singing and cry aloud,
> you who have not been in travail!
> For the children of the desolate one will be more
> than the children of her that is married, says the Lord.
> Enlarge the place of your tent,
> and let the curtains of your habitations be stretched out;
> hold not back, lengthen your cords and strengthen your stakes.
> For you will spread abroad to the right and to the left,
> and your descendants will possess the nations
> and will people the desolate cities.

The Three Grades of Marriage

Times of dryness and of being forsaken by the Spirit shall be followed by times of marvelous fruitfulness of spirit. Again the time shall be, when the spirit of love and purity, of community and brotherliness, of justice and concord, shall be poured out over you. This spirit of oneness shall bring about mission. Then you will go out to the poorest people, to the lowliest and most oppressed, to proclaim to them the time of salvation and the justice of God's people.

Then will come the time of great fruitfulness. In the very midst of the time of decline, a new movement will arise in which throngs of people will come to the Father's house, to the justice of God's people, to the unity of the Spirit.

Isaiah continues:

54

> Fear not, for you will not be ashamed;
> be not confounded, for you will not be
> put to shame;
> for you will forget the shame of your youth,
> and the reproach of your widowhood you
> will remember no more.
> For your Maker is your husband,
> the Lord of hosts is his name;
> and the Holy One of Israel is your Redeemer,
> the God of the whole earth he is called.

Thus God will marry His people.[1] The forsaken woman is once more accepted by God; the material world will once again become the communion of the spirit and the flesh.

The marriage between God and His people becomes visible as a fellowship of justice, a justice for the wretched. This justice is not possible unless God becomes one with His people; unless the people, God's people, become His spouse. Just as a wife is devoted to her husband and surrounds him with the proofs of her love, so too the holy mountain will be fruitful. And the bridegroom will be a bridegroom of justice. And this justice will become visible. The city is now shown to be a city of open gates, of concord, a city with community of work and community of goods, a city of perfect love. That is the holy mountain.

This holy mountain cannot be attained unless the bridegroom of justice has made his dwelling in the city. He is beloved by justice; he is the one who protects justice on earth. There is no other justice than that of unclouded unity and community.

Let us believe in the bridegroom of justice!

[1] see Appendix

The Three Grades of Marriage

Then his justice will come to all those who dwell in the city. It will be evident that this justice is valid, not before men but before God. This is the justice that appeared with Christ Jesus in His living and dying. This is the first grade of justice: <u>our bodies are to be bound no longer by the service of injustice, but by the service of justice.</u>

The second grade of justice is that which results when visible justice springs forth from the marvelous justice of faith. Hand in hand, brothers work together to bring as many as possible in from out of the world, so that a loving throng may be assembled from this world and the third grade of justice may make its appearance.

Thus the kingdom of heaven is like a king who holds his son's wedding. The kingdom of heaven is compared to a wedding. There is no one who is uninvited. All are called, without exception. Not one is too pious to be invited. None is too godless to have been invited long ago. The bridegroom is the King of justice and the bride is the Church.

The bridegroom's friends stand and listen to him. When the bridegroom is present we must rejoice. We must pass on the joy of the wedding to people, we must bring them this news: <u>the hour of the bridegroom is now; the moment of his arrival is now. Repent! Christ wants to show himself.</u>

The Church must be brought to Christ as a pure virgin. The Church's task, therefore, is to wait for Christ in spotless readiness. A Church with the ultimate earnestness, with the holiest task, does not believe *in* people but believes *for* people, believes that the spirit rules over the body through the soul. This can take place only when God's Spirit commands the body.

The bright, pure raiment of the Church is the justice that has meaning in God's eyes. It is the justice of works, the justice that comes forth from the Church. Anyone who does not have this raiment of justice cannot take part in the wedding of the Lamb.

The Church does not consist in a gathered people, a people who by the strength of their hands have built up a communal life. The Church does not consist in these people who are brought together. The Church is the Jerusalem above, the mother of us all. We recognize this final fact in our faith in the Holy Spirit. We do not believe in a church that comes from human beings.

The Three Grades of Marriage 127

We believe only in a single, perfect Church that comes to us from God through the Holy Spirit.

This fact, that the Church comes to us, is the ultimate reality of community life. We confess openly that we would never have been able to remain together in community had we not experienced this hourly coming down of the Spirit. We are not important, but the Spirit coming down to us — this is what is important. This is not a subjective feeling on the part of individuals, a feeling in which they may be mistaken; it is the objective fact of the Church.

The Holy Spirit comes only where He gives the Church to men. There is no other coming than the coming in the unity of His Church.

Where the bride is, the bridegroom is. Where the city-church is, the Spirit is. The one and only way the city-church can come into being is through the Spirit coming to us.

God's kingdom is justice in complete fellowship, peace, and unity; it is joy in perfect love. God's kingdom does not exist except in the coming of the Holy Spirit.

We know that a community of will has been formed when these very results become evident in that community: the proclamation of truth, conversion through complete repentance, dedication in complete faith and complete love which becomes reality in the community of action.

The coming of the Spirit to the gathered people in community—we testify to this through the place of Christian marriage in the perfect unity of the Church.

MARRIAGE IN UNITY

WHAT DO WE have to bear in mind when two members of the brotherhood wish to marry? when a member wishes to marry someone outside the brotherhood?

We have to bear in mind one thing: the spirit of the Church of God's kingdom, the spirit of unity. There is nothing else to be considered. When the love of a man and a woman is fully dedicated to the spirit of the Church and stands under the rulership and direction of this spirit, serving the unity and brotherliness of God's kingdom, the only thing to conclude is that they should marry. When this unity in the spirit is lacking, but emotional and erotic attraction have arisen, the relationship should come to an end.

If real unity concerning a marriage is not present in the whole church-community, it should be reaffirmed that the Church stands above everything. In this question of marriage, the unity of the Church and of God's kingdom is more important than anything else.

Then there is the question of whether it is possible for brotherhood members to marry persons outside the church-community. If these persons are drawn by the spirit of the cause, by brotherliness and justice, and are won for the innermost faith and life of the spirit, they will no longer remain outside. Then the marriage will be a brotherhood marriage. But if the person outside the church-community does not seek a full, life dedication, then he or she cannot marry a brotherhood member. No one who lives in the full communion of all things, including spiritual values, can enter into a marriage bond which does not live in this communion. Such a marriage would stand in the way of one's faith and spiritual communion, and one's faith and spiritual communion would stand in the way of such a marriage. It is unthinkable.

All these questions have but one single answer, not a system of answers, not an artificial structure of thoughts and principles, rules and regulations, but one single answer: *unity!*

This word, unity, can be grasped only when one knows the spirit of unity, when one accepts

Marriage in Unity

for oneself this spirit of unity and accepts all that it brings, in order to live in accordance with it. This is the whole gospel of Christ for all creation.

The powerful message of God's kingdom is the mystery of the Church which is the Body of Christ, the mystery of the city on the hill, of the Jerusalem above. The whole truth is embraced in the one word: *unity*.

MARRIAGE A SYMBOL

NOW WE HAVE the joy of looking ahead to the tasks which are given to this marriage bond within the life of today's church-community. The present times are infinitely difficult, not only for this or that person but for many people. A very large number of human beings and families live in great need. Need has also come to us because of the particular circumstances in central Europe.

It is a decision of faith to form a marriage bond in such times. Faith is courage; it has no fear. We do not know what will happen to the individual in the future. It is possible that a small or large part of our number may suffer a violent death. It is also possible that some married couples, including the marriage bond formed today, may be suddenly and unexpectedly torn apart. Therefore, we rejoice all the more when a young couple are led together and we may

Marriage a Symbol

state: come what may, they are a married couple.

In today's world situation it is essential that here and there among men there continue to exist rays of light and hope, spiritual realities by which the unity of God's peace and the brotherliness of true justice are recognized. This is our only task. It is by no means our task to solve all the problems of the day. Ours is a much more straightforward and simple task. Our task is to represent unity in the midst of a disunited world; to live in friendship in the midst of a hostile world. Our task is to represent the justice of true brotherly love in a communal life in the midst of an unjust world.

It is a very great joy for us to have been allowed to found twelve marriage bonds at the Rhön Bruderhof and now a second marriage bond at the Alm Bruderhof, and to know that this friendship, this peace, this love, this justice, this unity will be clearly recognizable through these newly founded families. Particularly in a time of so much unrest we must realize that people will not like to hear our word. On the other hand, facts will always be recognized. We do not want facts that are extraordinary. We do not want to create a sensation. We seek the very simplest. For this reason our bond of baptism is such an extremely simple symbol, that of water. And for this reason our Lord's Supper and love meal are such extremely simple and plain signs, that of eating and drinking together. Now the unity between God and men is established in the very natural symbol, that of the marriage bond.

It is a very plain and simple fact that we are a bond, a uniting of families, in which unity and community and love rule between man and wife, between parents and children. Different families are bound together in full brotherliness and equality within the unity of the Church. The unmarried brothers and sisters belong to this bond of families in just the same way. All this is very simple and uncomplicated, and yet it is a very deep miracle. How many towns are there, where even a few families could unite in real unanimity and unity? How many church groups would be able to extend the unanimity of their song and prayer to a common life whose members could work and live together?

Yet the very thing the world needs is the replacement of bolshevism and fascism by a practical Christianity where true love and unity in

Marriage a Symbol

real community overcome all privilege and all injustice. By mentioning bolshevism and fascism we mean to indicate that what is entrusted to us is nothing sensational. It is something that lives and moves in all men. There is not a human being on the whole earth who does not have a longing for unity and community, for love and brotherliness, for peace and friendship and justice. The ideals of the classless society and unity of the peoples are in truth the ideals of all mankind. Every man feels in his secret heart this innermost goal of unity.

It is for this very reason that we have been placed in the midst of this world. We do not want to live in opposition to other men, set apart by an extraordinary gift. We are given the task of saying something very simple to men: <u>the life you really want to live, the life for which you long, has become the basic content of our whole life.</u> Because of this we have bound ourselves together in such a way that we can never be parted, even if the strongest political force were to be used on us. Our togetherness is indestructible. We have not given our word to each other but to God, because in our inmost being we feel and know that this way is the way for all men. This is the way community is lived in which people are held together and stay together, in which they hold together in unity and peace.

Your marriage bond stands as an image and symbol for this. You have given your word, not only to one another, but even more to God; to God and His Church! The faithfulness of your marriage bond is inseparable and indestructible because it is a faithfulness that comes from God, a faithfulness from God and toward God!

WHAT IS GOD'S LOVE?

W E WERE URGED toward a communal life by God's call to us. We all were moved by the questions of who God is, what He is like, and what He wills. <u>We believe that we have to live our lives in such a way that men may recognize who God is and what He wills.</u> It became a living certainty for us that God is love and he who abides in love abides in God.

But God spoke to us further and asked us what we understood by love. Then it became more and more clear and certain to us what God's love is, as distinguished from what is known among men as love. Fénelon[1] spoke of disinterested, unselfish love, but other philosophers have said that all love is egoistic and interested only in itself. We must admit that much of what is called love among men is nothing but selfish desire.

[1] French theologian, 1651 - 1715.

It is a little better if two people say, "We do not wish to go on living alone; we want to live selfishly together." This is what Fénelon calls "égoisme à deux" (the selfishness of two). It is still better if two people live for their children and grandchildren, but we should realize that this is still collective egoism. And thinking of the nation and of the sacrifices made by individuals and families for their country and for the people, we have to admit that this is a still higher form of love. Yet national and clan collectivism is merely a merging of many egoisms in a collective egoism. All these can be called love — family love, love of one's country, love in the sense of solidarity.

God's love is more than all these.

The community founded by God in Christ does not originate in the egoism of individuals or groups. The Bruderhof does not live for the Bruderhof's sake. We are not concerned with community for community's sake or for the sake of collectivism. We are concerned only with God's heart and the unity of His love.

In Christ, God has revealed His heart. Only if we recognize who Jesus was, how He lived and died, and what He wills, only if we really

What is God's Love?

recognize Jesus can we grasp what this means: God is love and he who abides in love abides in God, and God in him. The love that appeared in Christ does not seek the life of the individual nor the life in common. Christ's love seeks the meaning of life given by God. Christ's love seeks the calling and destiny of the life intended by God.

The Church is the place where we seek the ultimate meaning of our calling as revealed in Christ. We cannot express in a few words what this is. It is contained in the four Gospels. We can try to hint at it by saying that God is unity, and he who abides in unity abides in God, and God in him. We believe that God's whole creation with all its star-worlds and worlds of spirits shall become one.

If we look at Jesus' life we can see by contrast that this unity does not yet exist in creation. Sin is there. Sin is separation from unity. Satan and his demons surround the earth like an atmosphere. Jesus speaks quite plainly of satanic power. He calls this devilish power Mammon. You cannot serve God and Mammon. Do not gather treasures! Free yourselves from the cares of money! Property is Mammon, the devil. Its deepest root is in the heart of the devil. This root is self-interest and egoism, each man worshiping himself and setting himself up as a god. This is Satan: "You will be like God."[1] Therefore love, which is God, is the opposite of Mammon. Surrender yourself to that love which desires nothing for itself.

Jesus calls Satan the murderer from the beginning, as we read in John's Gospel. This means that all killing and murder is of the devil. Murder has its deepest root in the heart of the devil. Therefore the prophetic word in the Old Testament: He who sins, sins against life! It is God's character to create life; it is Satan's character to poison, cripple, and destroy life. Only that which destroys life is satanic and sinful.

God's love spreads life only, affirms all creative life, with this single exception: that we are ready to sacrifice our own lives for the lives of others. Such a sacrifice never means the destruction of other lives. The cross and the resurrection of Christ show us God's love, which redeems from all sin and death and unites all the separate elements of life. Christ died in order to destroy all divisions between the nations, to unite

[1] Gen. 3.5

What is God's Love?

all peoples. Jesus meets Satan in his stronghold — death. Death is decay and decomposition of life. God's love accepted death in order to reveal love and resurrection.

Jesus reveals Satan's destructive works of impurity and unfaithfulness in human relationships. He calls the demonic spirits which obey the devil, impure spirits. The Gospels tell us how these impure spirits destroy nerves and bodies. Destruction and impurity begin with man's imagination and permeate all his members. And what is worse, these spirits attack and disturb God's holy, creative order of marriage (in father, mother, and child), the very fountain of life. This is the worst: love itself, the very thing which men honor as love, is destroyed and made impure. Jesus opposed impurity and unfaithfulness with the purity and faithfulness of His love.

In the Sermon on the Mount Jesus confronts Mammon: To him who wants your coat, give your cloak also. He confronts the murderous spirit: Love your enemies. Confronting the impure spirit, He says: He who looks at a woman with impure thoughts has committed adultery in his heart.

When God's love is poured out in our hearts we are free from covetousness and from magnetic attraction and repulsion. Our community can not consist of the interaction of horizontal magnetic powers. True community arises when God's love comes down to us vertically from heaven. In such a community, love is absolutely pure, and marriage between two persons is a symbol given within the oneness of this community.

A further quality described by Jesus as a quality of Satan and his demons is lying. The devil is the father of lies, and all lying and deceit are of the devil. The spirit of God's love will show us His will. Unity and love in the church-community will be shown in the unanimity of her recognition of the truth. The *consensus fidelium* (unity of the faithful) is the characteristic of the church-community.

When the Holy Spirit reveals God's love, the knowledge of the church-community will concur with that of the apostles. Truth is absolute and has no trace of relativism. Truth has appeared in Christ; it comes to the church-community through the Holy Spirit; it unites all believers. This is the characteristic of truth.

Lying is error, deception, and insincerity as

What is God's Love?

opposed to truth and truthfulness. Truth is the substance and reality of life. Truthfulness is the characteristic of brotherly relationships in the church-community. Uprightness, an open heart in all relationships, a clear and definite admonition and a simple answer of yes or no, and no touchiness when admonished, but only joy— this is our truthful relationship. Therefore Jesus says: Do not use unnecessary words; do not speak untruthfully; speak shortly and to the point.

In the same way we could continue to speak of the King and of the kingdom of God, and the prince of darkness, the prince of this world. But this may be enough to show how God is love in Christ and in His Church. In short, our foundation is God's love, the love of Christ, the kingdom of God. It is the dominion of Christ given in the Church through the Holy Spirit.

LOVE REDEEMED

NO ONE CAN deny love; each one feels that love is his destiny; there is no life without love. If one looks into the mystery of nature's powers one sees that there is no life that does not exist in relationship with other life. Life is the union of all life; life is the bond between the living; it is the unity of the world of the living. Wherever we turn, all the forces of nature confirm this fact, even outside the world usually thought of as living. No matter which natural forces we look at, all of them are symbols of love and fellowship, of the joining together of everything that lives.

The natural forces of attraction and gravity swing immense constellations in rhythmic rotation around their central point. These characterize the powers of nature, the essence of nature, and at the same time the life of love. Warmth, electricity, radiation, and attraction of every kind, all these serve to materialize, to represent and symbolize the very principles of nature: the warmth of light, the light of love, love's uniting power that works and radiates in all areas of life. They all form one great unity. This is confirmed by the fact that energies can be converted and transformed into one another, so that the sum total of all energy in the universe is to be regarded as a constant quantity. This material fact is a characteristic and symbolic expression of nature's essence which is the essence of love: an unchangeable and unconquerable power.

Mankind's thinkers who have tried to disclose the essence of nature have again and again been struck by the fact that there is a power which is active in and on matter, an energy which shows itself as the essence of all things. All philosophers up to the most recent times have had to concern themselves with this problem. Whether we say with the pre-Socratic philosophers that everything flows, streams, floods, lives, and is in uninterrupted motion, or whether we confess with Schopenhauer that the secret of the world is the will, the impulse, the power of motion, we will find one and the same fact. The secret of the cosmos is the power that is revealed in movement and works upon matter and in space.

Nietzsche took up this primary principle and placed it in a new, important light. "What good does it do us," he asks, "to say with Schopenhauer that will is the secret of life, and the will to life is the driving force of existence? The will must always know what it wills. There is no will that is not clear as to the object of its willing. But what about life, I must ask, what is its worth, its content, its true secret, its goal? What is it that I want when I want life?" And he believed he was able to give us the answer to this question by claiming that "the will to power is the secret of existence."

Since Nietzsche we have had to re-evaluate this fact of existence. Nietzsche, a prophetic genius, foresaw the condition in which we find ourselves today, and yet in his vision of the men of the future he lacked the decisive factor. Will to power is said to be the secret of life. Which power is meant, then? What, then, is the power that has lasting value? Which power is to fill my life? Shall it be the power to rule, to heap up possessions, or the power to oppress and enslave others; the power of violence, which asserts its existence and enlarges its possessions only by robbing others?

Love Redeemed

If Nietzsche meant that, and sometimes it almost seems so, then we feel with innermost certainty: That is false! That is death! That cannot be life! Life that enslaves and conquers other life, kills and exhausts it, despoils and exploits it, poisons and corrupts it, despises other life—that is not life, it is not the strength and power of life! Never! A life that lacerates, destroys and deprives of rights, is decadence, self-destruction and degeneration!

The will to power we mean is a different force from that of possessiveness and slavery. It is the power of love, and love is stronger than death. The basic driving force of love is the will to life which is the will to love; it is faith in the power of love. The unifying force of life does not try to poison; it is the power of love, the power that forms relationships and community.

All the partitioning and uniting we see in nature is aimed at this. Whether it is propagation of the species, the love of the sexes, or mutual help and service of one species to another, we see that the first principle is not the struggle for existence. On the contrary, it is the will to community, the primary relationship of interdependence, the innermost connection with one another, the help to one another, the unity of all consciousness, the unifying of all living things, the love of all living things for one another. Life in nature reveals that love is the essence of life. All the splendor of color and harmony, all rhythm has its high point in love.

Love is the heartbeat of life. It is born out of the fulness of life, its exuberance and joy, and is begotten in strength. It is the superabundance of life, and only that life is living which is capable of exuberance. That life is love which has within it overflowing life. Love is the spirit's rejoicing in what is real. This power of unfolding life in love is the highest activity, the supreme joy in creating, the creative power in the unfolding of all energies.

Just as in flowers and birds, so also in men, the times of love are times when body and soul are penetrated by the spirit, times of activity and heightened powers. When love comes to the one for whom it is destined, it will take hold of him and lead him to the full expansion of his powers, thus making him fit for work within the community of men. But only he can love who himself stands firmly on his feet. Weaklings are poor lovers. Love can appear only where life

Love Redeemed

pulses strongly, and when in such a person life comes to its unfolding, all onesidedness and eccentricity are overcome. Love is life, an exultant *yes* to life, an exultant *yes* to community of life. That alone is love.

When I hate I take something away from myself. Life is a continuous enrichment of existence through the overcoming of all obstacles to life. Life is struggle and overcoming, but life is eternal power and overcoming in the sense that death and killing are overcome by the healing, exuberant force of life which is love. The death of life, the murder of life, is the primary sacrilege against life; it is the antithesis of love and of the will to community.

Anyone who believes that he must kill, out of love and solidarity and faithful devotion to the beloved one, destroys by his own act the very object of his enthusiasm and devotion, namely life itself, the community of life. No life remains in the killer, for "whoever takes the sword must perish by the sword." This is obvious when love for one's country or solidarity in the class struggle is misunderstood; but it is just as true of a misunderstood love of the sexes.

All that murders, possesses, holds on to rights

and conquers them; all that enslaves and corrupts bodies, that kills enemies, that drains and exploits sexual love: all this is death to life, is denial of community, is desertion of love, is emptiness of spirit, spiritual suicide and godlessness.

True love is the indissoluble oneness of all that lives. Coming from the Spirit, which is the all-embracing oneness of life, the life power penetrates the movement and joining of souls and leads to physical union in marriage and to the common work.

True love is spirit, is power. By spirit we mean not the sharp logic of human intellect, not the threads which the human brain spins; that also belongs to the spirit, but spirit is more than that. It is life, it is love. Spirit is the power that binds to community, it is the life-unity of the cosmos, it is a bond and a band, it is a circle and a ring, rhythmic movement around the center. Spirit is unity.

All this, however, is often not clear to us when we speak about love on the erotic level, for our language no longer distinguishes between the love of the spirit, of the soul, and physical love devoid of soul and spirit. The Greeks knew this distinction deeply. They knew the covetous de-

Love Redeemed

sire of love, knew the emotionally stimulated Eros; they also knew Agape, the love inspired by the Spirit of the living God.

There are many people who in their inner scepticism have come to the point where love has no meaning for them outside the physical and sensual. It remains a fact that in the divisions of the brain the spheres of religious perception of life and of the feeling for community are located near and related to the sphere of erotic relationships; thus in the life of man these communal experiences of love are filled and flooded with the joy of the senses in the bodies of the loved ones. Love that comes from the Spirit, that is directed toward the whole, that is not aimed at covetous possession, is always present where there are human beings. But possessive desire which wants the body for the body is just as much present. And between the two lies the great, wide, deep area, that of the emotional life.

Just as our inner life is the battlefield of mighty forces, so this area is the scene of violent struggles. The struggle for existence, the covetous will, spring from our self-centered ego. These forces are always there, and their power working in us is simply the principle of evil. For me, evil is simply that which is hostile to life; and great and divine is that which brings true life, which furthers and increases life. The arch-enemy of life is the covetous will, the business spirit of Mammon, the legal spirit of property relationships, the detachment of sexual desire from the soul and from the unity of the spirit, away from community of spirit.

All this is death; it is no longer connected with life; it is decay. He who goes to the prostitute becomes one flesh with her without being one in spirit with her; he has defected from his own soul; he has separated himself from his own life connection; he has become the murderer of his own life. Whoever in greed holds fast to his own possessions, even while his inner self urges him and the will of his spirit drives him to find common life and work and fulfilment with all that is living, is a murderer and devastator of his own life and the life of his fellow men.

Love alone is life. Only through love is life redeemed. But love itself must be redeemed, for we are diseased in our love. Our love is degenerate, our souls corrupt, our spirit dispirited.

Love Redeemed 153

And just for this reason the faith that there can be community among men is lacking. We no longer believe that there can be community in the Spirit. We no longer believe that community can go so far that all property and belongings could be held without any right to possession. We no longer believe that love can be redeemed from possessiveness and greed and that love can bind a community of men in the solidarity of all life relationships.

I say we no longer believe in this, and yet we all do believe in it. Just this is the strength in our innermost being, that in the deepest depths of our hearts this faith lies dormant and cannot be killed. This source of faith and hope, of life and love, lives triumphantly in us all. We could not live at all if we no longer had this faith. It may be buried, withered, or distorted; it is always there. In us all lives hope in the future, will to community, joy in the future unity of life. The spirit of love's energy is in everyone; it is present in every human being.

But this spirit is not only present in us, it is in the whole world. It comes over us in certain moments of exaltation and with such urgency and force that we are overwhelmed and thrown to the ground by it, so that all doubts vanish like soap bubbles, and we feel: all this is reality, this love, this faith in the unity of mankind, the certainty that all that is living belongs together; this is real and actual truth. Pilate asks Jesus, "What is truth?" and He answers, "I am the truth!" We all know this in those decisive hours when we become true and truthful and stand face to face with eternal truth.

There is one solidarity between men. We are all equally guilty of our division, of the need that burdens us at this moment of history, and we are all equally driven by eternal truth to deeds of mutual love and surrender. We feel there must be community again! It will be a community of work, a creative bond, a fulfilment of love, a unity of life.

Those who turn their thoughts away from this world and set their hopes on a life after death are counterfeiters of truth. *To us* the new redemption is to come; here on earth the new will shall be done. Only through the love from God can we be freed from the love that leads to death. Only through the love which is life can we be freed from the love which is death.

Many have gone before us in this, Jesus being

Love Redeemed

the first and most decisive. It was bound to happen that this Man, being so different, was murdered. That He was murdered by the military, by the best legal state that ever was, by the greatest prophetic people that ever lived, by the leaders of the church and the voice of the people, all this cannot be accidental. We all are the murderers. Mankind murdered Him because the greedy will to possess, the covetous desire of possession and holding on to possession was too strong to be able to tolerate this Witness of truth.

And still today we cannot bear His truth, and so we twist it every way possible and no longer have the courage to make the meaning of the words, "Love your enemies" clear to ourselves. Everything that He showed is contained in the simple words, "What you wish that others would do to you, do that also to them."

I have met many pious people who were very much concerned about the souls of their fellow men, but I observed something quite astonishing about these people. They had no eye for the need of their starving neighbors, although they knew quite well what they needed for themselves and for the health of their own bodies. I never could understand how such people could confess themselves to Jesus with big words. We go the way of Jesus only when we leave everything in order to go with Him. That means standing up for all men, and first of all the oppressed. This is how He himself lived, and this is how many people have conducted their lives in the course of the centuries.

The nineteenth century distorted the image of Jesus in an amazing way and we are now in a crisis; our actions no longer fit our words about God. Those who call themselves atheists bear witness to the future of love, to solidarity with the deprived and dispossessed; those who call themselves Christians mostly hold to the possessors and wish to preserve the *status quo*. In earlier centuries not only individuals such as Francis of Assisi but throngs of people hastened to help each other in mutual fellowship.

In this materialistic age we see that the commandment Jesus gave us in His Sermon on the Mount, "Strive first for the kingdom of God and His justice, and everything else shall be yours as well," has not gripped Christendom. The coming revolution will have to be the overturning and re-evaluation of all values, the revolution of all revolutions.

Love Redeemed

It is clear what revolution is: the opposite of evolution. Certainly it belongs to development in a sense, but only as a sudden leap in a slow walk, like an unexpected crevice in a level mountain path. It is the pressing upward to new life of suppressed strata, an historical overturning which brings forth to the light everything that lay in dusk on the shadowy side, deprived of love and light. The important thing is whether such an overturning helps what was previously undeveloped and suppressed to reach its development. The true revolution must be such that through it comes the brotherliness of men toward one another.

Brotherliness can arise only out of the spirit of brotherhood; it will not come about unless the starting point and the goal and the means of fighting are led and determined by this spirit of brotherhood. Therefore I confess to this revolution, the most decisive and deepest revolution of all: the enormous world catastrophe of which Jesus knew, the overturning of all things and of all relationships among men. He called it the coming kingdom of God.

Jesus saw and felt that this coming of the living God among men was the highest that men can attain, that is, that they *become men*. Those very people who long for the unity of life; who have only the simplest human kindness as the content of their lives, the will to life, the joy in all living things, solidarity and brotherliness—these are the ones who are at all times the most oppressed. This is precisely the reason that so few people are ready to enter through this narrow gate, simply to become children in this small community, on this narrow way, simply to go with Jesus; for such a decision means the loss of all privilege and property of every kind. It means that we must perish, that we suffer a social downfall so serious that most people feel it is direct suicide. And in a certain sense it is. Jesus put it into words, "He who loves his life will lose it; but he who loses his life for my sake will find it."

We have to lose it in order to find it. This fact means that our corrupted love life is overcome, it means that we are freed from the love of possessions, from covetous desire. It seems like dying, but it is a dying to rise again to new life so that we win through to the true life, so that we come from death to life. We win through not to an otherworldly, heavenly life, but to physical life on this earth. The life about which the early Christians testified, our bodies shall be temples of the Holy Spirit, this life is on this earth. Together we shall become a real unity, a growing church-community, an organism; the world shall become a consecrated place for the spirit of community. Such a community shall be a community of work, for the Spirit always seeks out matter. And what arises in the new life of the growing church-community shall be the simple man. Brotherly men conceive of brotherhood and community of goods as the vital force of life-unity which embraces all things and renders possible a truly just distribution of all goods of life and work. The humane man must again come out of oppression to leadership.

We are infinitely far away from this goal. We have to trust in the spirit of life which is the spirit of love and unity and solidarity; trust in the spirit of life and justice which alone is life. In this trust we shall attain, through freedom and beyond equality, to brotherliness and true love.

CHRIST THE HEAD

CHRIST THE HEAD IN THE GOSPEL OF MATTHEW

JESUS IS THE HEAD. Christ is the Head. What does that mean? First of all, at this word everyone will have the feeling that Christ is the commander, Christ is the ruler, Christ is the king. All that is true. But it is not quite the same as what is meant by that word — Christ is the Head.

The head is always there to recognize the truth and to express it. In the head are the eyes, the ears and the other important senses to perceive things as they are. At the same time the head gives the possibility of recognition, the possibility of thinking out and understanding the truth. Certainly one can carry such a picture too far. One cannot apply every detail of an illustration to the thing itself. The head is not

Christ the Head

the same as the intellect. Even in nature that is the case. And it would be an even bigger, a far worse mistake to equate Christ as Head with the intellect. Up to a point one can make a comparison with the mind or reason of the human head. But the Spirit of Christ is not the same thing as human reason. Christ the Head is the bearer of the Spirit. He is the bearer of the revelation. He is the bearer of divine truth. That is not the same as reason or intellect; we are all aware of that. They are comparable with one another only to a certain degree.

We shall see from the Gospel of John that Jesus, who is the truth, is the essence of things. His truth is the life-kernel of all things. His truth is life. That is more than the intellect of all mankind. At the same time, Jesus is the teaching of divine truth. He is the master of truth. Jesus is the teacher who reveals God's truth and God's Spirit. Therefore He is the Head. What revelation is can be indicated quite simply as the word. The word of God is the revelation of God. It is simply this: God is love.

Because God is love, He wants to come out of himself. He wants to show himself although He is invisible. Because God is love, He wants to announce himself. Because God is love, He wants to speak out what is in Him. A closed person is not a loving person. God cannot be closed. He is open, open-hearted, open-minded. Therefore He wants to reveal himself. He wants to give a message. He wants to proclaim the gospel. He wants to say what is to be said. <u>Everything that has ever been said out of God's will to love, the love by which He wants to make himself known, is fulfilled in Christ.</u> Therefore Jesus is the Word that became flesh. The word is the concern of the Head. Therefore Jesus is the master and teacher of God's word, and all who follow Him are His pupils.

When we speak of the disciples of Jesus, we should never forget that the original, simple meaning of the word "disciple" is nothing other than "pupil." The disciples of Jesus were the pupils of Jesus, and they were brothers to one another. Therefore Jesus says in Matthew 23, verse 8, "One is your master, and you are all brothers." (By the way, no husband should be master over his wife; Christ alone is that.) This being a pupil, however, does not mean a literal learning of the lessons which Christ has set down. Therefore, what we said before about intellect must be said again about being "pupils." It is a comparison and the comparison is important, but it must not be applied in an exaggerated way to every little point.

In Matthew 12. 49-50 we see who His pupils are, that is, those who do the will of His Father in heaven. "One is your master, you are all brothers." Now He says who are the brothers: Because you are all pupils of one master, you are brothers; therefore none of you can be master over another. So it is that man and wife are brother and sister. The Hutterian Brothers speak of their wives as their sisters in marriage. Now Jesus says here, "My brothers are those who do the will of my Father." This shows that being a pupil of Jesus is not a purely intellectual thing. To learn the truth from Jesus means to do the truth and to live in it.

Now Jesus goes on to say, in the Gospel of John, "For this I have come into the world, to bear witness to the truth." He says this at a very decisive moment, just as He is being condemned to death. So this is the King — Christ; this is the Head — Christ. He is the one who reveals the truth and reveals it in such a way that it is done.

This can never mean that Jesus is an absolute ruler with material power. He is no tyrant. What He is, is said at the end of John 18 in verse 37. "You say that I am a king. For this I was born, and for this I have come into the world, to bear witness to the truth." In this way He becomes the true king of all His realm. One who is a child of truth hears Christ's voice and follows it. The nature of the Head, the nature of Christ the King of His realm, is that truth comes forth from Him; that this truth arises in those whom He teaches. In this same way the husband should live as the head with his wife. Whatever he says out of the truth of God arises at the same time as truth in his wife's heart. This calling to be the word leader is shown in Christ himself with utmost perfection. As the Head of the revelation, He speaks the truth in such a way that none of it is lost. "Heaven and earth will pass away; my words will never pass away."[1] This means that Jesus the Head never takes back a word of the revelation. Jesus never alters a word that He has spoken as bearer of the Spirit, for His word is the whole, the essential truth.

Now if the Spirit of Christ, coming down from

[1] Matt. 24 . 35

Christ the Head

the Head, descends upon us as members of His body, then in our circle too Christ who is the Head can never contradict himself. He cannot say one thing to one member and the opposite to another. Nor in marriage can He say one thing to the man and another to the woman. His word does not pass away. His word does not change. Man and wife can represent contradictory things only if at least one of them shuts his heart to the Holy Spirit. For Christ wants to put the same unchangeable truth into the hearts of both.

It is not true, then, that the man with his apostolic task is in a superior position to the Mary-like wife. The man is not the leader of the woman; he is her word leader. He gives expression to that which is living in her also. The deepest source of this relationship is clearly seen in Matthew 11.25. "I thank thee, Father, Lord of heaven and earth, for hiding these things from the learned and wise, and revealing them to the simple." Thus the truth, which is the task of the head, will not be given to especially clever and superior men. Otherwise, any man would have to be so much afraid to be a servant of the Word in the church-community that he would have to refuse the service. No man would dare to become a husband. Rather, we see man as head in the same way as we see Mary and the Church, which is the womanly nature. It is not the intellectual reason in man's commanding brain that is receptive to the truth; it is his childlike spirit. The man must be of childlike spirit if he is to receive the truth.

The way Jesus teaches His pupils is quite different from the way a too-clever university professor teaches his pupils or the way a statesman does it. Jesus does not seek to make His pupils clever or masterful men; He seeks to make them childlike people. "Thou hast revealed it unto them who are not of age, unto children." Therefore Jesus says, "Here is a child. Be like children; this is the only way you can enter into God's kingdom." But the childlike spirit is and remains spirit, which is authority and revelation.

Jesus goes on to say in what sense He is the Head, namely, "Everything is entrusted to me by my Father; and no one knows the Son but the Father, and no one knows the Father but the Son, and those to whom the Son may choose to reveal Him."[1] Over everything the Head has

[1] Matt. 11.27

Christ the Head

the authority of the Spirit. Only in Christ is the Father recognized. The Head as bearer of the Spirit must reveal the Father. He is the thought, the mouthpiece and the word of the Father; in this way He reveals the Father. Therefore He is the Head; that is His nature and character. He reveals the Father in such a way that this revelation makes no one proud and overbearing; it only makes people childlike and simple. This fact, witnessed to in Matthew 11 — that the truth is revealed only to children and simple people — is crucial in the discipleship of Jesus.

Jesus' word of truth is the Spirit of the Head; therefore His word is always different from the intellect, is always more than the intellect. Jesus' truth is heart and life. The truth of Christ the Head is the revelation of God's heart, of God's living breath.

An extremely important passage in this direction is to be found in the story of the temptation of Jesus. "Man cannot live on bread alone; he lives on every word that God utters."[1] Therefore the word of the Spirit must never be taken literally or in a purely rational way. Here we are talking about God's life breath. We are talking

[1] Matt. 4.4

about the living word which proceeds from God at this very moment.

God's breath is the life-breeze which blows directly from Him now. It is not a matter of repeating words spoken by Him six hundred years before Christ or thirty years after Christ's death. The breath of God is something that is revealed now and directly. This is why the Brothers of Reformation times spoke of the living word as that word which comes to us *now* directly from God.

Man lives, then, by all these words that come to men from God's living breath. Here is the fact of life with which Jesus begins His course. "Man cannot live on bread alone; he lives on every word that God utters." This is the revelation by which He conquers the tempter Satan. The secret of Christ the Head is that out of the word comes true, God-given life, and that this word is the living breath of God, who is coming to us now. Because of this Jesus says, "This truth is life; this truth is light."

Jesus says of himself, "I am the light of the world." We know that He also said, "I am the way." The Head recognizes that the direction in which one must go is light and life. His way

Christ the Head

means knowing the goal and knowing the direction one needs to go to reach the goal. The truth and the life in Jesus is that He shows us the way to go; even more, He *is* the way we must go. Also, we cannot go the way in the dark. Jesus is the light of the way. "You are light for all the world; a city that stands on a hill cannot be hidden. When a lamp is lit, it is not put under a bushel measure; it is put on the lamp-stand, where it gives light to everyone in the house. And you, like the lamp, must shed light among your fellows, so that, when they see the good you do, they may give praise to your Father in heaven."[1]

That is how it is. The Head who illuminates everything, being bearer of the Spirit, is bearer of the light for the whole world. And this light shall shine for all men. The Head, who is the light-bearer, wants the Father's will to be revealed, wants the Father's heart to be revealed, "so that they may give praise to your Father!"

We see that this revelation of the Father, going out from the light-bearer, is not a human intellectual and rational revelation; it is a life-bringing revelation. Verse 16 says expressly,

[1] Matt. 5.14-16

"when they see the good you do." Work belongs to the revelation of truth. Jesus on the cross says of His work of truth, "It is completed." The work is completed. The truth is revealed. Because of this Jesus says, "I have come into this world to reveal God's work." He came to destroy the works of the devil. He came so that God's will might be done. He is the revelation of the word and of the work; this revelation goes out from the Head, the Spirit-bearer. We see this in Matthew 13 . 54. He taught the people in their meeting houses in such a way that they said in astonishment, "Where does He get this wisdom from, and these miraculous powers?" This is what the Jews asked in regard to Jesus: How is it that such wisdom and such deeds are given to Him? Jesus the Head makes the people marvel at His deeds as well as His wisdom.

The revelation of the Head, then, is not merely what we usually understand by a teaching. We see this also in Matthew 20 . 26-28. Here it becomes clear what Jesus' work is, what His deed is; how completely different His influence is from that of the humanly great teachers. "Among you, whoever wants to be great, must be your servant, and whoever would be first must

Christ the Head

be the willing slave of all—like the Son of Man; He did not come to be served, but to serve, and to surrender His life as a ransom for many."

So Jesus is not the Head so that He may be a tyrant. Never! He can never be that. As surely as He is the Head, so sure it is that He is no despot. He wants to serve. In service He wants to give His life. He gives His life so that men may be freed. He makes all men free. Thus He also makes woman free, truly free. The freedom He gives her is not an emancipation from the creation appointed by God; it is the true freedom, which God and His creative Spirit gives her. He gives her the freedom of the spirit given by the revelation of God. He gives woman the motherly freedom which He gave Mary. This is the redemption of woman.

Thus the head, bearer of the Spirit, never rules over woman tyrannically. The head is the lowliest servant of the body. This is a wonderful paradox. The word leader is the lowliest servant of the Church. This is no exaggeration. It is the truth.

Before Jesus' disciples were taught by the Holy Spirit, each of them wanted to be great. Each one thought he could be the first. "He sat down, called the Twelve, and said to them, 'If anyone wants to be first, he must make himself last of all and servant of all.' Then He took a child, set him in front of them, and put His arm round him. 'Whoever receives one of these children in my name,' He said, 'receives me.' "[1] You shall be children. You shall welcome children. You shall have children, for then you have me. This is something very crucial. It goes against the arrogance of the proud man and very definitely against the arrogance of the proud woman.

The same truth is expressed still more sharply in Luke 9. 46 - 48: "A dispute arose among them: which of them was the greatest? Jesus knew what was passing in their minds, so He took a child by the hand and stood him at His side, and said, 'Whoever receives this child in my name receives me; and whoever receives me receives the One who sent me. For the least among you all — he is the greatest.' " Did this thought, the question who was greatest, come from God? Certainly not! This thought of who was greatest was not from God. In the same way, the thought of rivalry between man and woman — which of the two is the greater — is

[1] Mark 9 . 36 - 37

Christ the Head 173

not from God. The spirit of this thought is a false spirit. The whole question does not come from God. The woman must not fear that the man may be the greater, otherwise she is not a true woman; nor must the man fear that the woman may be the greater, otherwise he is not a true man.

Jesus put a child into their midst and said, "You must wish for one thing only—to be the least of all." Thus Jesus wants the childlike spirit. In the childlike spirit we are to become true women and true men. The childlike spirit stands in contrast to the spirit of childishness. Yet it is also the spirit of power, the spirit of authority. This is shown by Jesus' words when sending out the apostles. "Full authority in heaven and on earth has been committed to me. Go forth therefore and make all nations my disciples; baptize men everywhere in the name of the Father and the Son and the Holy Spirit, and teach them to observe all that I have commanded you. And be assured, I am with you always, to the end of time."[1]

This is Jesus' last testament. You know it, but in this context you should receive it even

[1] Matt. 28. 18-20

more deeply into your hearts. Jesus is the Head. To Him authority is given. Authority is something different from force; it is the authority of the Spirit. Just as one speaks of the authorized ambassador of a state, so here the most perfect ambassador of God's kingdom is spoken of. "Full authority in heaven and on earth has been committed to me." This is the spiritual authority of the Head.

This authority leads to the making of pupils. "Therefore go and teach all people, make all people my pupils." The Head and teaching belong together. It is lamentable that Jesus is so little understood in His teaching. He is often understood as the redeemer who forgives sins. He is seldom understood as the teacher who reveals the truth.

We recognize in the example of Mary the true nature of woman; now all the more we recognize, in the example of the apostle, man and his task. His is the apostolic task. "Go out and gather! Gather for me disciples, pupils, from all nations. Lead them through baptism to the community of the Father, the Son, and the Holy Spirit and teach them to follow all that I have commanded you. For see, I am with you always, to the very

Christ the Head 175

end of the world. Teach all people. Submerge them in the atmosphere of God, in the life of God the Father, the Son and the Holy Spirit."

When the apostles accepted the teaching and their mission, this meant that they did what Jesus said. It is the apostles' task to lead to this obedience of faith. This is the task of the word leader; it is the task of the husband for his wife and children. It is the task of teachers, both men and women, and of the sisters who work with the smaller children in the church-community. Women are in no way excluded from this task in its innermost sense, but it is in a special way the task of the apostolic man.

The promise which the apostles need for this task is the promise that Jesus himself will remain with them as the Head. They can certainly not do it in their own manly strength; Christ's presence is necessary. Man can take this task upon himself only from the authority of Christ, the Spirit-bearer.

The word leader of the church-community is not in himself the head of the Church. Christ is the Head of the Church in the clarity of the Word and the direction of the way. But the word leader has to represent this Word which is Christ.

And this is what the husband has to do in marriage too. Therefore one can and must say that the man is the head of the woman. He is the head, not in himself, but in Christ. It must not be taken literally, as though man were the overlord; it must be accepted deeply in the atmosphere of the Spirit. Otherwise something quite terrible would surely come about. But in the true Church, which stands under the true leading of the Holy Spirit, it will become something God-given. Then Christ can come into His own.

CHRIST THE HEAD IN THE GOSPEL OF JOHN

Jesus Christ is the Head of the Church. Jesus Christ is the revelation of truth as it has appeared in Him from God's heart.

The Gospel of John is an especially deep-going statement of this fact in Jesus Christ. At the same time, the way it is expressed is so unusually simple, that it helps one to be alert to grasp the depth of these simple words.

To begin with, let us try to understand the first five verses of the first chapter of John. In the beginning of all things the Word was already

Christ the Head

present. The Word was closely united with God; yes, the Word was divine in nature. In the beginning the Word was closely united with God. All things were created through the Word; nothing has come into being without its power. The whole of creation was filled with its life, and this life is the light of mankind. The light is still shining now and always into darkness, for it has not been overpowered by darkness. It is the Word which has made and formed all things. It is the Word which proceeds from God and has God's nature. It is the expressed thought of God and the inmost meaning of His heart. That which has become Word is God's innermost being. The Word is the revelation of God. It is, therefore, the creative Word, for God wants creation. God is love. That is why He needs objects of love. He has to create a world in order to be able to love it. This has happened in Jesus Christ, who is the living Word.

This Word, therefore, is life. It could not satisfy God to create a dead world. He had to create a living world so as to be able to love it. For this reason Jesus Christ, who is the living Word, the Word of God the Creator, creates life.

The life of plants and animals could not satisfy

God either; certainly not. Undoubtedly they too have a soul and can feel, even plants. But it is not clear whether or to what degree plants and animals have an inward light in which God is revealed. Therefore we read, "That life was the light of men."[1] The revelation of the Bible, the word of God through the prophets and apostles, distinguishes between men on the one hand and animals and plants on the other hand; whereas some human religions confuse the world of men so much with the animal world that they place animals and men on one side and plants and minerals on the other.

But Christ, who is the revelation of God, is Head over man. He gives light to all men. There is no man, not even among the peoples "outside Christianity" or in the thousands of years before the birth of Christ, who has not received light through Christ. This is expressed in the ninth verse — "The true light enlightens every man." Therefore, not only is there a mysterious unity between those known as Christians, those who read the Bible or have heard its words; there is a unity between all men, whether they are called Christian or heathen. There is no man who has

[1] John 1.4

Christ the Head

not received light from Christ. It is another matter, of course, whether and to what extent men follow this light.

Even before Jesus was born, He was at work as the Head, the mind of God, the light of God. This is the decisive faith of early Christianity; otherwise the historical Jesus would be no more than Buddha or Zoroaster. According to the faith of early Christianity, the historical Jesus is the eternal Christ, and as such He is the manifestation of the divine light which has shone at all times. There exists, then, a pre-Christian Christianity, a Christianity outside Christianity proper. And frequently atheists have more light from Christ than those who always carry a Bible around with them. In other words, He lights all men who come into this world.

The Word became flesh so that this perpetual light which is given to every man might be shown even more clearly. "So the Word became flesh; He came to dwell among us, and we saw His glory, such glory as befits the Father's only Son, full of grace and truth."[1] The Word became flesh — this is the majesty of God in truth, in which the greatness and clear splendor of God

[1] John 1.14

and the whole force of the streaming light of His love is made plain to us; the Word became flesh that we might know for certain what God wants and what His greatness is. Jesus came into the world to proclaim the Father.

"No one has ever seen God; but God's only Son, He who is nearest the Father's heart, He has made Him known."[1] God is absolutely invisible. But Jesus proclaims Him, wholly and completely, and therefore Jesus is the Head, the spoken thought of God. "He who sent me to baptize in water had told me, 'When you see the Spirit coming down upon someone and resting upon him you will know that this is he who is to baptize in Holy Spirit.' "[2] The expressed thought of God is not intellect, but spirit, and the Spirit is upon Jesus. Thus Christ is the Head. This is the mystery of His life. He is the Head in which the Holy Spirit lives. This Head is inspired by the Holy Spirit. All His thoughts are revelations of the Holy Spirit, and all His deeds are revelations of God. In Him, God's greatness and majesty, God's heart and God's love, are revealed. All this appears in Jesus. Thus in the eleventh verse of the second chapter

[1] John 1 . 18   [2] John 1 . 33

Christ the Head

we read that "This deed at Cana-in-Galilee is the first of the signs by which Jesus revealed His glory and led His disciples to believe in Him." At the wedding in Cana He revealed His glory as God's greatness and majesty.

In the third chapter, Jesus' contact with a seeking, questing man—Nicodemus—comes up for the first time. This is the same revelation of God. In the second verse Jesus is greeted by Nicodemus as "master" and "teacher" who comes from God. " 'Master,' he said, 'we know that you are a teacher sent by God; no one could perform these signs of yours unless God were with him.' " The Head is the Master and the Teacher and therefore He is the one who performs God's work. As such He answers Nicodemus, "What I teach is life; it is spirit."

This life must become completely new, and therefore it must begin just as small as with the smallest children. Because it must begin pure, it must begin small. This is the new birth from the spirit. "In truth I tell you, no one can enter the kingdom of God without being born from water and spirit. Flesh can give birth only to flesh; it is spirit that gives birth to spirit."[1]

[1] John 3 . 5

This new life must therefore spring from the Holy Spirit, in whom Christ is the Head. And so this new birth does not happen in the interest of the individual person, but in the interest of the kingdom of God, in which Christ is the Head. This is said at the end of the third verse. "Unless a man has been born again he cannot see the kingdom of God." He cannot even understand it! And at the end of verse five, "No one can enter the kingdom of God without being born from water and spirit." He has no part in the Kingdom. It does not come to him in any way. He does not enter it.

The kingdom of God shall and will reveal God's complete love and complete unity. For this, man must be born anew; otherwise he cannot grasp it. He cannot have the least part in this Kingdom. For this new birth and for this coming Kingdom Jesus, bearer of the Spirit, is the Head. He is the Word and the spokesman for the Kingdom. He is the thought and the witness of the Kingdom. He is the witness for all that He has seen of God and His kingdom, which others have not seen at all. In chapter 3, verse 11 we read: "In very truth I tell you, we speak of what we know, and testify of what we

Christ the Head

have seen, and yet you all reject our testimony."

New birth comes about in Christ through the same Holy Spirit who sees the kingdom of God and will rule over it. The all-creative thought of God is more than the thought that fills the human head. The thought of God is life-giving spirit. Jesus the Head is filled with the life-giving Holy Spirit. The living character of this Spirit had to be explained to ignorant men by means of images. That is why Jesus speaks of the living spring water of the Spirit. That is why He speaks of the blowing wind of the Holy Spirit. In Jesus the Head, everything is in constant living activity. The Holy Spirit is always living and creative movement. "Whoever drinks the water that I shall give him will never suffer thirst any more. The water that I shall give him will be an inner spring always welling up for eternal life."[1] Fresh, flowing water, living water, the springing well of water, spring water — this is the image of the Spirit. So we read, in chapter 7, verse 38, "If a man believes in me, as the Scripture says, 'Streams of living water shall flow out from within him.'" The streams of living water are the powers of the Holy Spirit,

[1] John 4 . 14

are the thoughts of God; but just because of this, these thoughts, which are God's power, are much more than human thoughts. It is the Holy Spirit himself who thinks in the hearts of the believers who are born of Him; He thinks the thoughts of God. It is the Holy Spirit himself who, coming from God, fills and moves the hearts of believers. He fills the whole Church.

Woman is in a special way an image, a symbol of the Church, filled with the Holy Spirit. The word leader and the apostolic man are given to the Church in a special way in order to express God's thoughts in a guiding way, as thoughts and powers which work and live in all members of the Church (and so, naturally, in woman too) though often unspoken.

Worship in spirit and in truth, as well as the leading of the Word, is a matter for the whole Church, just as the expression of truth, through her spokesman, is the task of the whole Church. The revelation which Jesus the Head brings is the revelation of true worship for the whole Church. "But the time approaches, indeed it is already here, when those who are real worshippers will worship the Father in spirit and in truth. God is Spirit, and those who worship

Christ the Head

Him must worship in spirit and in truth."[1] The followers of Jesus whom we call the disciples came to Jesus and said, "Teach us to pray." Jesus would not have been the Head if He could not have shown them according to the Spirit how to worship God in spirit and in truth. For if God's kingdom is love and unity, it is above all the uniting of men's hearts with God's heart. Therefore worship and prayer, which is a uniting with God, a uniting put into words, is of the utmost importance for the revelation of truth. For God will come down to man when we call Him, in order to take all things and all members under the rule of His love.

For this we are asked to declare ourselves ready. He wants to be unmistakably called to come to us. He wants to recognize the spirit in which we approach Him in its true nature. It is not a matter of many words in saying the prayer which Christ teaches us to pray; it is a matter of the spirit in which we come before God. That is why people who come together to worship and to pray "in spirit and in truth" must be completely one in spirit and in truth. This we see in the words, "But the time approaches, indeed it

[1] John 4 . 23-24

is already here, when those who are real worshippers will worship the Father in spirit and in truth."

When the Church has become unanimous in the unity and the truth of the Spirit, when she has recognized the will and nature of God in unanimity, truthfulness, and objective clarity, the immediate and definite result is that God's will is done. It is done through the power of this same Spirit in which God is worshipped. In fact, we must say that the real supply of strength, the true food for new life is given just as much or even more through action as through prayer. The head takes in nourishment for the whole body. The head recognizes what has to be done. With Jesus himself, as the Head, action was the decisive factor. His action, as well as His word, was the revelation of God's will. His strength was the doing of God's will. "Jesus said to them, 'It is meat and drink for me to do the will of Him who sent me, until I have finished His work.' "[1]

If the doing of God's will is the strength and food for the completion of the work, we have found a new answer to the question put by Tol-

[1] John 4 . 34

Christ the Head

stoy, "What do men live by?" Life is action, movement. We live by doing the best, by doing the will of God. Jesus lives by doing God's will. The doing of God's will is His existence. The doing of God's will is His nourishment. His life comes from doing God's will. Thus His whole life work arises from God. In this way He, the thinking, Spirit-filled Head, executes the whole work of God. He does it for all men by drawing all men into this work, by stimulating them to it just as much as they will allow themselves to be moved by Him, to be animated by Him.

We have seen that the Head sees with the Spirit, as the human head sees with the eyes. Jesus does what He sees. He sees what the Father does. From this, His action arises. Only those who see God and see God's work can do His work. Jesus could do nothing without perceiving the work of the Father. Thus He says to us too, "Without me you can do nothing." Unless you see God's kingdom you cannot do anything for God's kingdom. You must recognize the kingdom of God as it is; unless you do, you cannot live for it. You must recognize Jesus if you want to recognize God's kingdom. And if you see God's kingdom, then you will live in accordance with it. Then your own will will not matter to you any more. Only the will of the Father will matter to you. "I cannot act by myself; I judge as I am bidden, and my verdict is just, because my aim is not my own will, but the will of Him who sent me."[1]

As it is with action, so it is also with speaking. For the word is action if it is really truth. Word, deed, and truth proceed from the head. That is why Jesus says, "When you have lifted up the Son of Man you will know that I am what I am [the Messiah, the Head, the King]. I do nothing on my own authority, but in all that I say, I have been taught by my Father. He who sent me is present with me, and has not left me alone; for I always do what is acceptable to Him."[2]

Jesus does nothing by himself; He speaks what the Father teaches Him. This is again what we have seen and said several times already: Jesus is the Head. The Head is filled with the thoughts, with the Spirit of God. Jesus says what God tells Him. Thus Jesus brings God's revelation to all of us. He does not bring us the revelation of God as a book religion, as the

[1] John 5 . 30   [2] John 11 . 28-29

Christ the Head

Koran, for example, would do; with Him everything is the faith of the Spirit. Therefore Jesus says, "The Spirit alone gives life."[1] The Spirit, who lives in the Head, descends upon us from Him and gives us life. His word comes to us in the Holy Spirit. So does the word of the Bible. For the Holy Spirit spoke directly to the prophets and apostles. In the same way the word comes to us, here and now, as the direct breath of the living God, but always in complete accordance with the word of Jesus, of the prophets and of His apostles.

The word and life of Jesus is the strength-giving food for a life that does God's will. "I am the bread of life."[2] Jesus is the living word through the life-giving Spirit. This living, active word is absolutely true. Therefore it must also express the truth concerning what is bad and evil. "The world cannot hate you; but it hates me for exposing the wickedness of its ways."[3] The world hates Jesus because He tells the world that its works are evil and destructive.

The clear discrimination of good and evil, of life and death, is the concern of the Head. With Jesus, evil and good mean the same as dead and

[1] John 6 . 63   [2] John 6 . 48   [3] John 7 . 7

living. Evil is everything that leads to death. Good is everything that creates true life, life in the divine sense. That is why Jesus continues, "The teaching that I give is not my own; it is the teaching of Him who sent me."[1] It is of God, for it is God's life, and therefore it is God's teaching. This teaching must be expressed clearly and acted upon clearly. For this, a clear mind is necessary. And this all-illuminating Head is Jesus.

We too are led to recognize and to represent this clarity. There is only one way to recognize the truth. Not the intellectual way of reason, but the living way of action. This way is to do what we know through God and to know God through what we do because of Him. However much we might study theology and know Biblical words, if we do not *do* what we have seen, we will never be clear. "Whoever has the will to do the will of God shall know whether my teaching comes from Him or is merely my own."[2]

Just as the doing of God's will is and remains the food, the source of strength, so the doing of God's will is the only possible way for us to know the teaching of Jesus. His will can come about only if we do it. All of us have experienced

[1] John 7 . 16   [2] John 7 . 17

Christ the Head

this when we have called upon God and Christ and His Spirit to come. We are then concerned with life. Jesus is the Head for the whole of life. He is the light for the whole world. He gives light for the whole of life in order to bring the whole world to the right way of life. This is the task of the Head for the whole body. "Once again Jesus addressed the people: 'I am the light of the world. No follower of mine shall wander in the dark; he shall have the light of life.' "[1] Just because Jesus is and remains the light of the world in God, He is never by himself. Wherever He is, there the Father is who sent Him. For He is the Head, filled with the thoughts, filled with the Spirit of God. "Here am I, a witness in my own cause, and my other witness is the Father who sent me."[2]

From this we also see the truth expressed in the next verse. "They asked, 'Where is your father?' Jesus replied, 'You know neither me nor my Father; if you knew me, you would know my Father as well.' " He who knows Jesus knows the Father; for Jesus the Head is the knowledge of the Father. Everybody who feels something of God listens to Jesus. "He who has God for

[1] John 8 . 12 [2] John 8 . 18

his father listens to the words of God. You are not God's children. That is why you do not listen."[1]

He who is of God hears God's words. Jesus spoke words of fundamental significance about this in the wonderful chapter about the good shepherd. Word and voice belong to the Head. "The sheep hear His voice ... the sheep follow because they know His voice .... My own sheep listen to my voice; I know them and they follow me."[2] To be able to recognize and distinguish Jesus' voice is a wonderful thing. Whoever is truly touched by the Spirit of Jesus Christ can distinguish His voice from any strange voice. The most precious experience in the life of the church-community is this: Christ speaks. It is the certain knowledge, the experience of feeling that now the living word comes to us, now His Holy Spirit is speaking. This is why we are now so united; this is why we now feel so sure; this is why we now go to work. The alien voice is rejected. No other head is recognized than Jesus Christ. He alone knows the Father. He alone brings the heart of the Father. He brings the thoughts of the Father.

[1] John 8 . 47   [2] John 10 . 3, 4, 27

Christ the Head

Jesus' life and death reveal what is in God. We know Him by the fact that He gives His life without taking the lives of others. He who gives his life for his friends without taking the lives of others is on the way of Jesus; he reveals the nature of God. "I know my own sheep and my sheep know me — as the Father knows me and I know the Father."[1] In the Gospel of Matthew Jesus puts it this way: Know the false prophets by their wolfish natures. True prophets reveal that the nature of the lamb is to sacrifice his life. Thus Jesus shows us the love of the Father who sacrifices for us the best the Father has. As the Head, He reveals the deepest thought of the Father by giving His life for His enemies. In His life and His death and in the power of His resurrection He revealed perfect love as the power of God. When Jesus came to the dead Lazarus, Martha, the dead man's sister, said to Him, "Lord, the air is foul by now; he has been four days dead." "Why," Jesus said to her, "have I not told you that if you have faith you will see the glory of God?"[2]

In Jesus we see the majestic glory of God's all-conquering love. Thus in Jesus the name of

[1] John 10 . 14-15   [2] John 11 . 39-40

God is revealed in radiant light. The task of the Head is to reveal the nature and power of the Father. In the twenty-eighth verse of chapter twelve we read, "A voice sounded from heaven, 'I have glorified it [the name of the Father] and I will glorify it again.'" The nature and the name of the Father is love. God is love. And he who remains in love remains in God, and God in him. Thus Jesus' whole attitude shows ministering love as the sole power of His life. We see this in the service of love that He did when He washed the feet of His disciples. "I have set you an example: you are to do as I have done for you."[1] The Head bends down to wash feet! This is Jesus, and by this we too shall be recognized, if we are truly His disciples. We practice love when we bow our heads and render the lowliest service to one another, such as washing each other's feet. Ministering love is the characteristic feature of discipleship of Jesus. This is the way. This is the truth. This is the life. "Jesus said to him, 'I am the way; I am the truth and I am life; no one comes to the Father except by me.'"[2]

How can men come to have a share in this

[1] John 13 . 15   [2] John 14 . 6

Christ the Head

life of the Head? Through the same Holy Spirit who fills the Head. The whole Head is full of the Holy Spirit. The Head sends this Spirit to us who are His body, and He sends it into all of this body.

"If you love me you will obey my commands; and I will ask the Father, and He will give you another to be your Advocate, who will be with you for ever — the Spirit of truth. The world cannot receive Him, because the world neither sees nor knows Him; but you know Him, because He dwells with you and is in you."[1]

"Your Advocate, the Holy Spirit whom the Father will send in my name, will teach you everything, and will call to mind all that I have told you."[2]

"When He comes who is the Spirit of truth, He will guide you into all the truth; for He will not speak on His own authority, but will tell only what He hears; and He will make known to you the things that are coming. He will glorify me, for everything that He makes known to you He will draw from what is mine.... A little while, and you see me no more; again a little while, and you will see me."[3]

[1] John 14.15-17 [2] John 14.26 [3] John 16.13-14, 16

The Holy Spirit goes out from the Head and fills the whole body. He teaches all the truth of the Head and recalls all the words spoken by Jesus. Thus He leads us from the Head into the whole future of God's kingdom. This is the object of the Head. This is the object of revelation. This is the object of the Holy Spirit. This is the object of God's thinking. Therefore it is the object of action and of life.

When the Holy Spirit comes upon us, the result is that we love Jesus and keep His word.

"In truth, in very truth I tell you, he who has faith in me will do what I am doing; and he will do greater things still because I am going to the Father. Indeed anything you ask in my name I will do, so that the Father may be glorified in the Son. If you ask anything in my name I will do it."[1]

"Anyone who loves me will heed what I say; then my Father will love him, and we will come to him and make our dwelling with him."[2]

"Dwell in my love. If you heed my commands, you will dwell in my love, as I have heeded my Father's commands and dwell in His love."[3]

"This is eternal life: to know thee who alone

[1] John 14.12-14   [2] John 14.23   [3] John 15.10

Christ the Head

art truly God, and Jesus Christ whom thou hast sent."[1]

In these last words, "This is eternal life..." we see once again that it is a matter of life. This life is the true knowledge. Life and knowledge are one. Here is no life without knowledge, and here is no knowledge without life. <u>This is life — to know God and Christ.</u> It is the task of the Head to have knowledge and to proclaim knowledge. It is the task of the whole body to be completely imbued with this knowledge and thus to live in accordance with it.

The seventeenth chapter consists of the prayer with which Jesus turns to the Father. He is the Head because He has revealed God. He is the Head because He has made the cause of God radiantly clear. In the fourth verse we find, "I have glorified thee on earth by completing the work which thou gavest me to do." Only by making God clear and bright to all believers could He finish the work.

"I have made thy name known to the men whom thou didst give me out of the world. They were thine, thou gavest them to me, and they have obeyed thy command."[2]

[1] John 17.3   [2] John 17.6

Thus Jesus revealed the name of God, that is, the character of God. He did this through His words:

"I have taught them all that I learned from thee, and they have received it: they know with certainty that I came from thee; they have had faith to believe that thou didst send me."[1]

Jesus made it known that the essence of God is the revelation of love. "I made thy name known to them, and will make it known, so that the love thou hadst for me may be in them, and I may be in them."[2] The Spirit-filled Head reveals the truth as the revelation of love. "Consecrate them by the truth; thy word is truth."[3] And the Word sanctifies the whole of life; it is the consecration of the whole of life. "Consecrate them by the truth; thy word is truth." This is the apostolic mission. This is the mission of the Head. "As thou hast sent me into the world, I have sent them into the world."[4] The life of the whole world has to be consecrated to this truth.

"For their sake I now consecrate myself, that they too may be consecrated by the truth.... May they all be one: as thou, Father, art in me,

[1] John 17 . 8   [2] John 17 . 26
[3] John 17 . 17   [4] John 17 . 18

Christ the Head

and I in thee, so also may they be in us, that the world may believe that thou didst send me. The glory which thou gavest me I have given to them, that they may be one, as we are one."[1]

The apostolic mission of the Head as shown in the above words of Jesus is recognized by the unity of the Church. Without the unity of the Church there is no apostolic mission. Thus we recognize that Jesus is the Head, because He came to bear witness to the truth. " 'You are a king, then?' said Pilate. Jesus answered, '"King" is your word. My task is to bear witness to the truth. For this I was born; for this I came into the world, and all who are not deaf to truth listen to my voice.' "[2] Therefore He could say on the cross, " 'It is accomplished!' He bowed His head and gave up His spirit."[3]

This is the final humility in the revelation of ultimate love — the bowing of the head in sacrificial death. In accomplishing the final task which He as the Head had to do, He bowed His head and died. But to His disciples He said after His resurrection, "Receive the Holy Spirit!"[4] Receive the Holy Spirit for the for-

[1] John 17 . 19, 21-23
[2] John 18 . 37-38
[3] John 19 . 30
[4] John 20 . 22

giveness of sin, for apostolic mission, for the authority to pass on the forgiveness of sin, for the unity of the body, for the life of truth and love which the Spirit of the Head has given to you.

CHRIST THE HEAD IN THE LETTERS TO THE EPHESIANS AND COLOSSIANS

Christ is the Head for the knowing and the doing of God's will, for He bears the wisdom of the Spirit. Everything was created so that Christ might be the fulfilment of all. The revealed mystery is this: Christ is the Head over all rulership; Christ is the Head over all authority, the Head over all spiritual beings and all worlds. Christ is the revelation of the mystery of the future. Where He is, hope lives as the vision and expectation of God's future.

In Christ all things will one day be brought together. The complete and ultimate purpose of His will must in God's time become reality. We pray to the Spirit of revelation and knowledge that we may understand and await this. In this way we receive the strength of Christ the Head, ruler over all authority.

Christ the Head

Christ is the Head of all worlds. Yet He is in a special way the Head of the body; He is the Spirit-bearer of His Church so that this Church may be united in perfect peace. Christ in you! As Head of the body He penetrates the whole body with His thoughts. The Spirit in Him floods the whole body, the whole Church. The whole body is Christ. The Church is the new incarnation of Christ. As He received His first body through Mary, so He receives His second body in His Church. Therefore the Apostle says that His Church is the body of Christ which fulfils all things.

This is the remarkable mystery of marriage. The man is likened to the Head. The Head is Christ, the bearer of the spirit of knowledge. The woman is likened to the Church. The Church is again Christ. She is His body. She makes the physical body of Christ a living reality.

Thus we understand when Paul says, "It is a great truth that is hidden here. I for my part refer it to Christ and to the church."[1] We must distinguish in Christ, first, that He is Head over all princely powers and spiritual beings, and secondly, that He is Head over the body

[1] Eph. 5 . 32

which is the Church. Let us try to keep these two things separate while striving to understand the Letters to the Ephesians and Colossians. Yet we must remember that in the end the two must become fused into one. The difference is the same that we will find in the Gospels and in the Acts of the Apostles. It is the difference between the kingdom of God and the Church.

Paul sees the kingdom of God in the spiritual beings. He sees Christ the King as the Head. He does not see Him so much on the throne; he sees Him more as the Head. We saw that it is the Head who bears the thoughts of God. The Head bears the inspiration of the Spirit. The Head sees and hears what God is and what God wills, and the Head speaks and declares what He has heard and seen. Paul therefore sees Christ as King of His realm in the sense of the penetration of all things by the Spirit. He is the Head, the Spirit, and as such will enter and possess all things spiritually.

This is how the kingdom of God will be. The Church is the forerunner and the sign of this. The Letter to the Ephesians tells us in chapter 1, from verse 8 on, that in Christ "the richness of God's free grace was lavished upon us,

Christ the Head

imparting full wisdom and insight." Verse 9 says that "He has made known to us His hidden purpose—such was His will and pleasure." That is God's counsel. It is the decree of a very definite order, that in Christ everything is to be united under one Head. The mystery of His will is made known to us. This has come about according to the decree which He has made before all eternity, and which He will now carry out in the fulness of time according to a definite order. What is the goal of this decree? It is that all things, both in heaven and on earth, may be united in Christ under one Head. This is the wonderful mystery of God's wisdom, and this is our calling.

"In Christ indeed we have been given our share in the heritage, as was decreed in His design whose purpose is everywhere at work."[1] We see that this mystery is to be imparted to us through the Holy Spirit, to give wisdom to the eyes of the heart and true enlightenment for a just understanding. "I pray that God ... may give you the spiritual powers of wisdom and vision, by which there comes the knowledge of Him. I pray that your inward eyes may be illu-

[1] Eph. 1 . 11

mined, so that you may know what is the hope to which He calls you."[1] This is the task of the Head, but the Head in a spiritual sense, in the sense of the Holy Spirit.

As we continue to verses 21 and 22 we find that He is enthroned "in the heavenly realms, far above all government and authority, all power and dominion, and any title of sovereignty that can be named, not only in this age but in the age to come. He put everything in subjection beneath His feet, and appointed Him as supreme head to the church." Christ is the Head of all things. Let us say it again: Christ is the Head over all power and might, over every force and dominion, over everything which is exalted now and in time to come. Over all these things Christ is the Head, in the sense that He bears the Spirit. In this sense, as the all-embracing Spirit, He is in particular Head of the Church; for she is His body, which these other things are not. We are told in verse 22 that God "appointed Him as supreme head to the church, which is His body." The Church is the completion of Him who without end is completed in all the members of the Church.

[1] Eph. 1 . 17-18

Christ the Head

Now the Letter to the Colossians shall once more show us the Head over all spiritual powers. Here the same truths are expressed in different words. The concern is with the wisdom and insight of the Holy Spirit. This is not a matter for the understanding only, but for the whole of life; not, as we have perhaps often tried to understand it, in an almost intellectual way.

" ... we have not ceased to pray for you. We ask God that you may receive from Him all wisdom and spiritual understanding for full insight into His will, so that your manner of life may be worthy of the Lord and entirely pleasing to Him. We pray that you may bear fruit in active goodness of every kind, and grow in the knowledge of God."[1] This means that to live in this way and bear fruit in all good works is part of the power of this knowledge. "May He strengthen you, in His glorious might, with ample power."[2] This is the authority peculiar to His spiritual majesty. In this way He is the Head over us all. He thinks through the Spirit, He thinks for us by giving us His Spirit. In this way, He works through us.

We find this restated in verses 15 to 19 of

[1] Col. 1 . 9-10 [2] Col. 1 . 11

chapter 1. "He is the image of the invisible God; His is the primacy over all created things. In Him everything in heaven and on earth was created, not only things visible but also the invisible orders of thrones, sovereignties, authorities, and powers: the whole universe has been created through Him and for Him. And He exists before everything, and all things are held together in Him. He is, moreover, the head of the body, the church. He is its origin, the first to return from the dead, to be in all things alone supreme. For in Him the complete being of God, by God's own choice, came to dwell."

He is the Creator and spiritual Head of all things. At the same time He is in a special way the Head of the Church which is His body. He is the first-born who awakens every member of the Church to new life, the first-born from the dead. In all things He is to have pre-eminence. "Through Him God chose to reconcile the whole universe to himself, making peace through the shedding of His blood upon the cross — to reconcile all things, whether on earth or in heaven, through Him alone."[1]

Verse 16 says, "In Him everything in heaven

[1] Col. 1 . 20

Christ the Head

and on earth was created ... thrones, sovereignties, authorities, and powers: the whole universe has been created through Him and for Him." They are created through Him because, as the Head, He thinks and fulfils the creative thoughts of God. Creative thoughts are creative works. This is the mystery of the Head who is the Word. Wherever the creative Spirit is, there is the creative thought, the creative word, the creative work, the creative embodiment. It is so because of Christ. Therefore He is the Head. This extends to all things without exception, from spiritual beings to the material outward aspect of things. Because of this the end of verse 16 says that all things were created through Him and for Him. For the same reason verse 17 says that He existed before the creation of all things. He created them all as the creative Spirit or the creative Head who bears the creative Spirit. Through Him the whole world is kept in existence, and this is how we understand the second part of verse 17, "All things are held together in Him." This is how we understand the glory that is to come. This glory is the majesty, the creative, life-giving spiritual strength of God in Jesus Christ. The whole world is filled through and through with God's thoughts and powers, coming from the Spirit who fills the Head, and all things shall have their place in the order of love.

God's first and last thought is unity, because God's first and last thought is love. "It is He who has brought us the news of your God-given love."[1] The bearer of this thought of love is the Head—Christ. In Him dwells all the fulness of divine life in one body, physically, just as the Spirit of revelation dwells in Him who is the Head. "For it is in Christ that the complete being of the Godhead dwells embodied, and in Him you have been brought to completion. Every power and authority in the universe is subject to Him as Head."[2]

Christ is the Head over all spiritual principalities. By nature and origin He is already the Head. God has made Him the Head now. In other words, as far as God's ideas are concerned, He is the Head already now. But in relation to the material reality of a fallen earth and a fallen mankind, it is in the future that He is the Head. When, therefore, we are thinking of men of this present epoch, He is the future

[1] Col. 1 . 8   [2] Col. 2 . 9-10

Christ the Head

Head. In God's thoughts and powers He is the Head *now*. He is the Head now in God's heart and in God's Spirit. But in the nations of today He is the Head in the future. While Mammon holds sway in the world as it does today, Christ is not yet the Head. In the material reality of world economy He is the Head in the future. In so far as it depends on the governments of modern states, Christ is the Head in the future. The same is true of the deceitful structure of modern society. The same is true of the struggle between the sexes, between man and woman.

The Church is sent into the world so that Christ may be disclosed as the Head. This is the only way that this can be shown to the world today. The Church is the only way that Christ can be revealed as the Head—in her, the body.

Let us turn back again to the Letter to the Ephesians. At the end of the first chapter Christ is called Head over all things after being expressly named as the Head of everything that is to come. Then, at the end of verse 22 and in verse 23, it says that He is made Head of the Church now, at this present time. This Church is His body. She is the living body of this Head. Body and head are one life. Only a murderer severs the head from the body. Christ, who is the Head, and the Church, which is the body, are completely united, as surely as the head of your body is joined to your body. In oneness of life with Him the Church completes the Head.[1]

This conviction goes so far that it is said of the body, of the Church, that she is the Christ. Not that any one of her members could be the Christ; that is completely impossible. But the wonderful penetration of the whole body by the Spirit coming from the Head, this wonderful unity of the whole spiritual body which is framed together out of all peoples—this is Christ! This can be shown by many passages in the Letter to the Ephesians. Let us look at just a few of them.

First, in chapter 2, verse 22, "In Him you too are being built with all the rest into a spiritual dwelling for God." Furthermore, it speaks of "the unfathomable riches of Christ," to whom belongs the spiritual body of the Church which is built from all peoples. "To me ... He has granted of His grace the privilege of proclaiming to the Gentiles the good news of the unfathomable riches of Christ."[2] The power of the

[1] Eph. 1 . 23 [2] Eph. 3 . 8

Christ the Head

Spirit who goes out from Christ the Head is spoken of. "[May He,] out of the treasures of His glory ... grant you strength and power through His Spirit in your inner being."[1] "Now, through the Church, the wisdom of God in all its varied forms [shall be] made known to the rulers and authorities in the realms of heaven."[2] Thus the wisdom of the Spirit shall be made known to the whole cosmos through the Church. This can happen only through Christ Jesus, only through the Head, only through the bearer of the Spirit. "This is in accord with His age-long purpose, which He achieved in Christ Jesus our Lord."[3] All these things can come about only through the love and creative power of Christ, who bears the Spirit.

In chapter 3, verses 17 to 19 we find, "With deep roots and firm foundations, may you be strong to grasp, with all God's people, what is the breadth and length and height and depth of the love of Christ, and to know it, though it is beyond knowledge." Thus you are to come as members who are in yourselves spiritually empty, to "be filled with all the fulness of God."[4] The

[1] Eph. 3 . 16
[2] Eph. 3 . 10
[3] Eph. 3 . 11
[4] Eph. 3 . 19

love of Christ, the love of the all-embracing spiritual Head, far surpasses in its breadth, length, depth, and height all the bounds of knowledge that have been attained hitherto. This love is more than mere knowledge, and yet it is knowledge, for it means being filled with the fulness of God's Spirit.

The fulness of God brings living unity through love, and therefore it is said, "Be forbearing with one another and charitable. Spare no effort to make fast with bonds of peace the unity which the Spirit gives."[1] Those who stand with Christ the Head are concerned with the unity of Christ's body which is created by the Spirit. Paul testifies to this mighty truth in verses 4 to 6 of chapter 4: "There is one body and one Spirit, as there is also one hope held out in God's call to you; one Lord, one faith, one baptism; one God and Father of all, who is over all and through all and in all."

This is the mystery of Christ the Head. In chapter 3, verse 3, Paul says that this mystery has been made clear to him by a special revelation. It cannot be said clearly enough that this is the mystery of Christ. Christ cannot be known

[1] Eph. 4 . 2-3

Christ the Head

unless the mystery is known, this one mystery, that He is the Head who bears the Spirit for His one living body, for the Church; that He, the Head of the Church, will be King of God's kingdom at the end of all things. These are the two spheres of power contained in the one Head. This is the mystery of the Church which is at work today, and it is the mystery of the whole great future kingdom of God; that is, of both these spheres as conceived through the Spirit.

In man's mind the intellect seems to rule, but in the Head of Christ the Holy Spirit rules. This is the point of comparison and this is the distinction. Because of this it is said, "In former generations this was not disclosed to the human race; but now it has been revealed by inspiration to His dedicated apostles and prophets."[1] In verse 6 Paul stresses, in contrast to former times, the one very special aspect of this mystery, that is, that all peoples together as one body now build the one body of Christ in the Church. Thus all peoples are joined in one and the same promise for the future, in one and the same gospel, in one body, in one organism of the spirit. "Through the Gospel the Gentiles are

[1] Eph. 3 . 5

joint heirs with the Jews, part of the same body, sharers together in the promise made in Christ Jesus."

This is the strongest imaginable contrast to nationalism. The separate peoples of individual nations, the privileged Jewish people, and any would-be privileged heathen people within a so-called Christian nation — all these are now replaced by the one spiritual body of Jesus, drawn from all nations. This body is Christ incarnate in our present time. The next verses state this very plainly indeed. "To me ... He has granted of His grace the privilege of proclaiming to the Gentiles the good news of the unfathomable riches of Christ, and of bringing to light how this hidden purpose was to be put into effect. It was hidden for long ages in God the creator of the universe."[1] The mystery of the body of Christ, the mystery of the Spirit's organism — this is the unfathomable riches of Christ; this is the true nature of the mystery which from eternity throughout the centuries has been hidden in God, the Creator of all things.

We see in the next verse that this is now made known through the Church and is, in fact, made

[1] Eph. 3 . 8-9

Christ the Head

known not only to men and their nations, but also to all principalities and powers of heaven. This mighty event comes to pass through the Church. The same is expressed in the Letter to the Colossians. "He is ... the head of the body, the church."[1] It is the Head who bears the Spirit and reveals the truth. This happens in the following way: "In Him the complete being of God, by God's own choice, came to dwell. Through Him God chose to reconcile the whole universe to himself"[2] — the whole which shall fill everything, the fulness of the Spirit and of the cosmos, the fulness of God! This is the perfect union which is the mystery of Christ's body. The body is at one with itself. A body would not be a body without the unity of love and of life. The unity of the Church is simply that of life in Christ and in His Spirit. It follows that the Church is Christ.

This is true to the extent that the Church is present. As far as there is unity, so far Christ is there. Paul says that this "secret hidden for long ages and through many generations" is "now disclosed to God's people, to whom it was His will to make it known — to make known how rich and glorious it is among all nations.

[1] Col. 1 . 18   [2] Col. 1 . 19-20

The secret is this: Christ in you, the hope of a glory to come."[1]

The mystery is twofold. First, it is Christ in you. Secondly, it is the expectation of the glory and majesty of a final future. Christ in you — this is the presence of the Church. Hope — this is the future of God's kingdom. These two belong together in the Head, who is Christ. In this way the Church has community of life with Him. "And in Him you have been brought to completion. Every power and authority in the universe is subject to Him as Head."[2] The Church is not God's kingdom, but the Church carries and receives God's kingdom through the Head, who is Christ. The Church, therefore, is dead to all other spiritual powers which hold sway in the world in the absence of the Spirit of the Head. "Did you not die with Christ and pass beyond reach of the elemental spirits of the world?"[3]

These words are very important because they show that the Church, which has life community with Christ, is not subjugated by the spiritual powers which hold sway in this world. As the Church, we are not subjugated to the mammon-

[1] Col. 1 . 26-27 [2] Col. 2 . 10 [3] Col. 2 . 20

Christ the Head

ism in the world. As the Church, we are not subjected to this world's demand that we shed blood. As the Church, we are not subjected to the military service of this world. As the Church, we are not subjected to the official lying of present-day society. We are not subjected to the impure spirits of the world and its large cities. As the Church, we are not subjected to Satan and the demons of this world which rule the spirit of this world and are its god. For we have surrendered and submitted ourselves to the kingdom of the only true God. Our citizenship and our public responsibility belong to the Kingdom, because we are completely and solely dedicated to the Spirit who comes from the Head and penetrates us, His own body.

All this is not yet the kingdom of God. The Kingdom is still with God in heaven. We cannot turn this world, which is estranged from God's Spirit, either into the Church or into the kingdom of God; but it is the task of the Church to show to the world by a living example how God does this and will do it. Paul says that the kingdom of God does not consist in rules about eating and drinking; it does not consist in any ordinances or human decrees or in living up to human ideals. It consists in righteousness and peace and joy in the Holy Spirit. The Holy Spirit — this is Christ's body, this is Christ.

CHRIST THE HEAD IN THE FIRST LETTER TO THE CORINTHIANS

The Holy Spirit — this is Christ's body, this is Christ. We find this in the First Letter to the Corinthians. In chapter 12, verse 27, we read of this organism of the Holy Spirit: "You are Christ's body, and each of you a limb or organ of it." Here it is explained in detail how it is possible for men to form the body of Christ. Basically it is not men who form the one body simply by joining together in a human way; it is the Holy Spirit who builds the body out of these believing men. To the extent that the Holy Spirit possesses those men who are open to Him, He unites and organizes them in the unity of this spiritual body. How this happens is shown throughout the twelfth chapter and is explained in a very graphic way. Here we see the one Spirit who inspires the unity of the body. Here is the one Lord and Master. Here

Christ the Head

is the one Christ as future King of the kingdom; the one God who creates this body. The gift of the Spirit is here. Revelation of the Spirit is here.[1]

This wonderful working of one Spirit is very manifold and diversified in its absolute unity. However diverse, however manifold and various this power is, it always streams from the one whole and is always for the common good. Whether it is the all-revealing words of truth or the teaching of knowledge; whether it is a special gift of faith through special strength of faith, as for example for the daily care of the Church; whether it is the gift of healing body and soul, or the spiritual gift of prophecy; whether it concerns the guidance of the ship of the Church by spiritual discernment; or whether it is the gift of tongues and their stirring, spiritual interpretation[2] — throughout all the richness, diversity and multiplicity, this remains decisive: "All these gifts are the work of one and the same Spirit."[3] This one and the same Spirit comes from the one sole Head of the whole. Just as in our bodies the blood establishes unity of life between all the members, so in the

[1] I Cor. 12 . 4-7   [2] I Cor. 12 . 8-10   [3] I Cor. 12 . 11

body of the Church the Spirit is the unity of life and consciousness, the bond and union between every living member.

In our human bodies there are many organs and members[1] — hands, eyes, ears, and numerous other organs whose natures and tasks are unknown even today, and which have very diverse functions. No member or organ of the body can say of another member or organ that it has no need of that other, or that the body itself and the life of the body have no need of it. All members are and remain in one and the same life destiny, bound one to another for the same task in life. Verse 27 says of the body of the Holy Spirit, "You are Christ's body, and each of you a limb or organ of it."

Now let us consider a few of the chief tasks in the Church in the light of this likeness to a body. First there are apostles, then prophets, and lastly teachers. All these three services of the holy organism are possible only through the inspiration of the Holy Spirit, coming from the Spirit-filled Head of the body. In looking at the highly complex organism of the body, Paul asks in verse 29, "Are all [of us] apostles? all prophets?

[1] I Cor. 21. 12-26

Christ the Head

all teachers?" Shall everybody strive to attain one of these three particular services in the Church? To begin with, the answer is No. The way that can lead to the final answer is given at the end of the chapter, in verse 31: "And now I will show you the best way of all."

Now we come to the song in praise of love in chapter 13. Side by side with these three — apostles, prophets, and teachers — the three deepest things are now placed. "There are three things that last for ever: faith, hope, and love; but the greatest of them all is love."[1] Following this truly divine train of thought, there come the words, "Put love first; but there are other gifts of the Spirit at which you should aim also."[2] But remain mindful that they are undeserved gifts of the sovereign and ordaining Spirit. This is true of prophecy above all, for this spiritual gift concerns the future of God's kingdom and the inward nature of His heart. Love, however, is that gift of Christ's Spirit which is given to every member of the body since it is the main quality of the Head. Prophecy, on the other hand, is a special and very significant gift which must be given to every Church because it re-

[1] I Cor. 13 . 13   [2] I Cor. 14 . 1

veals the power to live according to God's heart and to the future plan of God.

Let us now, after having clarified all this in our spirit, recall in a final note the question about man and woman. To summarize once more: Woman should become like Mary, in the likeness of the Church. This Church is Christ, as His body and spiritual organism of the greatest diversity. Church is Christ. Thus woman should be like Christ, as the Church is. Woman is like the Church. The man, however, should be like the Head, filled and inspired by the Holy Spirit, appointed for the revelation of the spiritual will of Christ. The Head is Christ. The man must correspond to Christ as the Head. He must be like Christ as the apostles were like Him. Here we see man and woman as equals before God. Both are to become like Christ through the inspiration of the Holy Spirit, and yet the one likeness is to be very clearly and basically distinguished from the other.

APPENDIX

The best reference to the personal background of Eberhard Arnold, and the best description of the events of the community life of the Bruderhof are to be found in Emmy Arnold's *Torches Together*. Most of the chapters of *Love and Marriage in the Spirit* are translations of typed transcripts of shorthand records of meetings. Most of these typed reports were scanned by Eberhard, and he made corrections in his own hand. Some shorthand notes, however, were transcribed after Eberhard's death.

On the Rhön Bruderhof the brotherhood room was only about sixteen feet square, with a wood stove in one corner. The low-ceilinged dining room would seat forty or fifty people comfortably. The reader must visualize Eberhard speaking, without notes, in one of these rooms filled with high expectation but quite ordinary people, people who had put in a hard day's work on the farm or in the print shop, in the kitchen, laundry or school. Often a talk which began during supper in response to the question of a guest, would continue two or three hours as darkness fell outside and the lamps were lit, while one brotherhood member constantly circled the house knowing that the Gestapo was looking for reasons to destroy the community. Sometimes a discussion, begun by one serious question, would continue for several days. As a question came alive, it had the undivided attention of the whole household.

On August 24, 1934, Eberhard's oldest son, Hardi, was married to Edith Boecker at the Alm Bruderhof, in Liechtenstein. "The Mystery of Unity," chapter five, was a talk that was a part of the preparation for this wedding. Chapter six, "Faith and Marriage," was prepared for the civil authorities at the time. Four young Englishmen — a married couple and two young women — had come to know Hardi in Birmingham, and had become interested in the Bruderhof. They came for the wedding, and with the intention of joining the community. One of them was alarmed by the place the wife took in relation to her husband in the marriage ceremony and vows, and questioned it. The emerging discussion was recorded, and is printed here as chapters two

Appendix 227

and three, "On Woman's Calling," and "The Nature of Woman and of Man." Eberhard felt the question such a deep-going one in its Christian significance, that he spoke in further meetings over the next two days, and these talks form chapter seventeen, "Christ the Head." It was a deeply moving experience, not just for the new English novices, but for the whole circle. In just this way, the chapters of this book are different points of discovery in the life of the community.

* * *

Love Divine and Human appeared in 1920 as an article in a book called *Junge Saat: Lebensbuch einer Jugendbewegung.*

Eberhard Arnold was involved with that part of the youth movement which sought in earnest to rediscover the religious source and foundation of life. *Junge Saat* was one of the early publishing efforts of the Sannerz community out of which the Bruderhof movement sprang. Both the community at Sannerz and *Junge Saat* witnessed to the wave of longing for an affirmation of life and justice that stirred so many in the wake of World War I.

On Woman's Calling; The Nature of Woman and of Man. These two pieces stem from a time at the Alm Bruderhof, when a number of young people, both married and single, who had committed themselves to the life in church-community, sought to understand more deeply the relationship between man and woman and their respective places in the order of creation.

The Nature of Woman and of Man reproduces a meeting on September 1, 1934, during which Eberhard Arnold answered some of the questions which were raised during the open discussion.

....

Marriage and the State. On June 24, 1933, six months after Adolf Hitler came to power in Germany (Jan. 30, 1933), at a time when the question of the relationship of the church-community to the state had become particularly acute, a young couple celebrated their wedding at the Rhön Bruderhof near Fulda.

This talk, given just before the couple went to the civil registry office, is an interpretation of the writings of Peter Rideman on the meaning of unity and on the question of church and state.

....

Appendix

The Mystery of Unity was spoken in a meeting of inner gathering and prayer at the Alm Bruderhof on August 23, 1934.

....

Faith and Marriage. After a wedding held at the Alm Bruderhof on August 24, 1934, Eberhard and Emmy Arnold accompanied the young couple to Triesenberg to establish their marriage with the civil registrar and the administrative official, who was the Catholic priest of the town.

Eberhard Arnold presented to the officials a summary of a Hutterian writing on marriage, and after returning that evening he recounted that "the official registrar as well as the priest were in agreement with this writing. It was noticeable that the clarity and energy of this witness of marriage made quite an impression. It is only a short summary, but these few pages shed light on the main issue in this ceremony." *Faith and Marriage* is this summary.

....

Conscience and Responsibility contains excerpts from the chapter "The Conscience and its Healing" of a book entitled *Innenland* (Inner Land) published in 1936 by the Alm Bruderhof.

....

The Bond of the Spirit is a talk given on June 23, 1933, the eve of the wedding referred to in connection with *Marriage and the State.*

....

Responsibility, Desire, and Love is an essay written in late 1920. In 1928 the writer took up this same subject under the heading "On the Struggle of Young People in the Problem of Love" as a contribution to a volume commemorating the fiftieth anniversary of Friedrich Wilhelm Foerster. The concluding paragraphs of *Responsibility, Desire, and Love* are taken from this later publication.

....

The Promise; Engagement. These two pieces are extracts from meetings of the brotherhood at the Rhön Bruderhof, taken down in shorthand. The meetings are held among the members much as a husband and wife or a family might gather to face questions and concerns that arise from day to day. The members are fully committed to the life in church-community and meet in the trust and faith that they will be led as one heart in their decisions.

The Promise reproduces a meeting held on December 28, 1934. *Engagement* contains words

Appendix 231

spoken by Eberhard Arnold on two occasions, July 15, 1933, and July 14, 1934. In spite of the difference in time it was felt that the two belong together under one heading.

....

The Three Grades of Marriage. This talk was given on July 25, 1931, and is based on a chapter "Concerning Marriage," of Peter Rideman's *Confession of Faith.* The latter is a translation of Rideman's *Rechenschaft,* written in prison in 1545, which was published by the Plough Publishing House in conjunction with Hodder and Stoughton in England in 1950.

The transcription of the sentence which we have translated as, "Thus God will marry His people," reads in the German, "So will Gott seinen Sohn sich vermählen." The shorthand notes of this talk in July 1931 were only transcribed in 1964. There were gaps in this transcription where we have supplied missing words in a few instances, and in this one case we have taken the liberty of changing a word, "Sohn" to "Volk."

....

Marriage in Unity. In August 1935 the brotherhood at the Rhön Bruderhof received a letter from a guest concerning questions of discipline and order in the community. This letter was read and discussed in a meeting of the members. *Marriage in Unity* is part of that discussion and was spoken by Eberhard Arnold at the close of that meeting.

....

Marriage a Symbol is a talk given on the occasion of a wedding that took place at the Alm Bruderhof, on May 19, 1935.

....

What is God's Love? At a meeting with several guests on August 2, 1934, Eberhard Arnold answered their questions by the talk reproduced in this chapter.

....

Love Redeemed is a lecture Eberhard Arnold gave in Hannover, Germany, in 1923.

....

Christ the Head. This teaching was given at the Alm Bruderhof on September 2 and 3, 1934, in answer to a discussion with new members of the church-community. Eberhard Arnold deeply considers his theme on the basis of the Gospels of Matthew and John and of the Letters to the Ephesians and Colossians as well as to the Corinthians.

GLOSSARY

Alm Bruderhof
> located in Triesenberg, Liechtenstein, from March 1934 to March 1938.

Anabaptists
> were prominent in Central Europe in the Reformation, forming the radical wing of the Reformers; their principal centers were in Germany, Switzerland, Moravia, and the Netherlands. The Anabaptists were widely persecuted because of their advocacy of adult baptism, of the separation of church and state, and of far-reaching social and economic reforms. Many thousands gave their lives in the persecutions they suffered at the hands of both the Catholic and Protestant churches and the state. They refused to take oaths, taught that obedience to the state was evil if it conflicted with conscience, and some refused to bear arms.

Brotherhood
> the members of the church-community in full unity and dedication. see Appendix "The Promise; Engagement" page 230.

Brothers
> see Hutterians.

Bruderhof
> in German, literally a place where brothers live. The name given to the communities of the Hut-

terian Brothers and the Society of Brothers.

Church-community
> a group of people, married and unmarried, living together voluntarily, holding common property on a Christian basis.

Eisenach colony
> Ziegelwald was the name of the colony located near Eisenach in Thuringia, Germany, where a venture in community living took place around 1934.

German Civil Code
> *Buergerliches Gesetzbuch* (*B. G. B.*) enacted in Germany on January 1, 1900. Contains 5 books and 2385 articles, regulating the relations of debtors and creditors, property, inheritance, marriage and family.

Hutterians
> In Moravia a group of Anabaptists numbering about two hundred adults were in favor of unconditional non-violence and community of goods in accordance with the spirit and example of the early Christians. In 1528 this group left Nikolsburg and found a place in the neighboring town of Austerlitz. Even before they reached their new home, they introduced community of goods: a halt was made en route, and the elders spread a cloak on the ground, on which everyone laid his possessions. From this group, after many struggles, emerged the distinct Church of the Brothers known as Hutterians, which still exists today.
>
> In the year 1533 Jakob Hutter became the fore-

most Leader of the Word among the Brothers, and they were named after him. In 1535 Hutter was captured while on mission journey in the Tirol, and on remaining true to his faith, after suffering brutal torture, was burned alive at Innsbruck, early in 1536. In the face of severe persecution, the group grew until it is estimated that by the end of the century they were as many as 70,000.

They lived a precarious existence marked by severe persecution and expulsion from their homes until in 1874 and 1877 they were forced to emigrate to the United States.

John Horsch, in his study, *The Hutterian Brethren, 1528 - 1931, A Story of Martyrdom and Loyalty* wrote: "Of the Hutterian congregations in Moravia it can be said that they were centers of true spiritual life and activity, of genuine Christian piety and devotion. It is not probable that at any time since the apostolic period the Christian ideal of brotherly love and entire consecration to the service of God was anywhere so fully realized as among the Moravian 'Anabaptists'."

Today there are over 14,000 Hutterian Brothers in the United States and Canada. Much the same life is lived in all Hutterian communities today as in the sixteenth century: full community of goods, communal work and worship, and a common table.

Rhön Bruderhof
  located near Fulda in Hesse, Germany, from November 1926 to April 16, 1937.

Servant of the Word
   see Word leader.

Werkhof community
   a religious-socialist venture in community living in Rüschlikon, Zürich, Switzerland, at about 1930, from which several members came to the Bruderhof.

Word leader and Servant of the Word
   It is important to grasp in a new way the meaning of leadership in the church-community. Leading usually takes place through suggestion or transference of the will of one to others. This can never be so with the church-community.

   Is any man able to occupy the place for the good in the hearts of others from his own strength of character or ability? Even if one had the best knowledge of human nature and the most complete experience, this would not be adequate. The answer is found only through faith in the Holy Spirit: we are united in deepest openness and obedience to the Holy Spirit. When we are united, when this is revealed to all, there must be someone to put into words and action that which is felt by all. This service is necessary for every area of life; everywhere whoever is responsible must be led by the Holy Spirit.

   The word leader is the spokesman for that which lives in the others. The word leader cannot speak or act out of himself. He says or does that which moves in the others and wants to be expressed in word or in deed. Never should there prevail a human leading. Everybody can be the spokesman for the life of the whole community. We have no principle of leadership and no majority system. We do not want one human opinion to rule over the others. We believe that the Spirit of truth manifests himself to all and never contradicts himself. We believe in the revelation of truth in the living community.

The service of the Word, appointed by God and His church-community, along with each member, has the special responsibility for the inner life of the church-community. He who has this task must first grasp the inward and outward situation of the whole group and bring it to clear expression in word and action. He must bring to expression that which is holy, which moves and fills the hearts of all, even if it is unspoken and undone.

> These thoughts are taken from a letter by Eberhard Arnold dated July 25, 1934.

During the last few years the communities of the Society of Brothers have felt a strong desire and a sense of urgency to share with all men the spiritual heritage that has moved and guided our life over the years. We have felt the wind that is stirring the times in which we live. This sense of urgency has moved us to take up again one of the tasks of the community in its early years in Europe—the work of the Plough Publishing House. We also long to be in deeper contact with others who are aware of the needs and suffering of our time, and who are working in one way or another to express their love and hope for their fellow men. We want as Christians to express our urgent longing and hope that all men on this earth will one day live in true justice and brotherhood under the rulership of God.

Torches Together: The Beginnings and Early Years of the Bruderhof Communities, by Emmy Arnold, tells the story of the first 17 years of the Bruderhof movement. It encompasses the time of the beginning, growth, setbacks, and struggles of the Bruderhof in Germany until the year 1937.

In *Eberhard Arnold*, Emmy Arnold briefly recounts the life of her husband, Eberhard Arnold. The book includes extracts from his talks, writings, and letters. Also included are some of his poems, several recollections written by friends at the time of his seventieth birthday anniversary, and a selected bibliography of writings about and by Eberhard Arnold.

Peter Rideman's *Confession of Faith* expresses the fundament of faith that has governed the life of the Brothers, known as Hutterians—originally an important part of the peace-seeking Anabaptist movement of the sixteenth century. The Confession, written in prison in 1545 by Peter Rideman, is indispensable to all who wish for a full understanding of the Reformation and post-Reformation periods.

Inner Words for Every Day of the Year, by Emmy Arnold, brings you a quote a day for a year from the writings of men such as Eberhard Arnold, the Blumhardts, Dietrich Bonhoeffer and others, who tried to put into daily practice their deepest faith regardless of the consequences.

Children in Community is a photographic essay. It is an intimate sharing of a precious part of our life in community with those who are interested, as well as a witness to what we feel about the education of children. It contains many pictures, poems, and stories by children, as well as short articles on the education of children by Eberhard Arnold.

There are other books available from the Plough Publishing House, including some pamphlets and paperbacks. A complete, free catalog will be gladly sent on request.

PRINTED AT THE OAKLAKE PRESS
Farmington, Pennsylvania